G000275225

Also by John Martin Robinson

THE WYATTS

THE OBSERVATIONS OF HUMPHRY REPTON

ROYAL RESIDENCES

GEORGIAN MODEL FARMS

THE DUKES OF NORFOLK

THE LATEST COUNTRY HOUSES

ARCHITECTURE OF NORTHERN ENGLAND

CARDINAL CONSALVI

OXFORD GUIDE TO HERALDRY
(with Thomas Woodcock)

THE COUNTRY HOUSE AT WAR

THE ENGLISH COUNTRY ESTATE

CHATTO CURIOSITIES: HERALDRY

TEMPLES OF DELIGHT

COUNTRY HOUSES OF THE NORTH WEST

TREASURES OF ENGLISH CHURCHES

BUCKINGHAM PALACE: THE OFFICIAL HISTORY

WINDSOR CASTLE: THE OFFICIAL HISTORY

HERALDRY IN NATIONAL TRUST HOUSES
(with Thomas Woodcock)

FRANCIS JOHNSON ARCHITECT
(with David Neave)

THE REGENCY COUNTRY HOUSE

GRASS SEED IN JUNE: THE MAKING OF
AN ARCHITECTURAL HISTORIAN

ARUNDEL CASTLE

FELLING THE ANCIENT OAKS:HOW ENGLAND LOST
ITS GREAT ESTATES

JAMES WYATT: ARCHITECT TO GEORGE III

REQUISITIONED: THE BRITISH COUNTRY HOUSE IN
THE SECOND WORLD WAR

THE TRAVELLERS CLUB: A BICENTENNIAL HISTORY

THE 6TH DUKE OF DEVONSHIRES HANDBOOK OF CHATSWORTH

WILTON HOUSE: THE ART, ARCHITECTURE AND INTERIORS OF ONE OF
BRITAINS GREAT STATELY HOMES

EX LIBRIS
JOHN MARTIN ROBINSON

Holland Blind Twilight

JOHN MARTIN ROBINSON

Foreword by

LUCINDA LAMBTON

Anthony Eyre

MOUNT ORLEANS PRESS

TO

HANNAH AND KATE

Frontispiece:
Bookplate designed and engraved by
Richard Shirley Smith

Published 2021 in Great Britain by
Anthony Eyre, Mount Orleans Press
23 High Street, Cricklade, SN6 6AP
https://anthonyeyre.com

CIP data for this title are available from the British Library

ISBN 978 1 912945 31 3

Printed in
India

Contents

OF FAME'

Foreword

READ AND RELISH this book; plunge straightway into it and savour every word. It is terrific; beautifully written by a saviour of so many of our buildings, who is also a wizard of scholarly originality and, to boot, an exceedingly clever character. It is jam packed full of important and making-you-cheer-out-loud discoveries and delights; what about the richly furnished underground pub belonging to the Architectural Press in Westminster? Resplendent with a stuffed lion given by Nicholas Pevsner, it could also claim to have Frank Lloyd Wright's signature etched into its mirrored walls. Beat that!

This is also a book that is laced through with quite brilliantly scathing social observations. Schadenfreude ahoy; what a pleasure it is to read spot-on and laugh-a-minute criticisms of those who most richly deserve it. A quite tremendous cast of characters is to be found within these pages: John Betjeman with his wife Penelope, Trevor Huddleston, Gavin Stamp, Colin Amery, Dan Cruickshank, David Watkin, Monsignor Alfred Gilbey *et al*; here they all are, paving the way for our greater happiness with their 'contributions of keeping alive the flame of English civilization'. Three hearty cheers for the glorious legacy of their work: Christ Church, Spitalfields by Hawksmoor had been a ruinous wreck for some fifty years before they painstakingly revived it—initially removing six tons of rubbish by hand—as usual with scrupulous scholarship. They also created umpteen conservation movements nationwide, from which we hugely benefit to this day. Let us sing the praises of the author's tireless work, as he so successfully storms through his ever more fruitful days, often clothed in the handsome perk of Lord Snowdon's great Uncle's morning coat—green with age and well over 100 years old. HURRAY!

LUCINDA LAMBTON
APRIL 2021

Christ Church, Spitalfields, before restoration with piles of rubbish cleared and burnt in the church yard by JMR and friends before the first concert.

I

Spitalfields

SPITALFIELDS WAS UNIQUE in London and indeed in northern Europe in the early 1970s for picturesque almost Asiatic squalor. Against a backdrop of decaying 18th century silk weavers' houses and the towering, blackened limestone hulk of the abandoned church of Christ Church Spitalfields, ravaged men in ragged coats tied together with string sprawled on the broken and ill-maintained pavements. Some drank cheap alcohol from bottles, others scavenged in the gutters for fruit and vegetables from the City market, then still in operation. The roads were strewn with mouldy oranges and rotten cabbages, until the sweepers and rats came out in the evening. On cold days the indigents crouched round little bonfires of burning cardboard boxes, paper wrappings, and broken timber crates retrieved from the market.

We, too, joined in the foraging for winter fuel in order to keep open fires going in the barely restored Georgian houses of a few sturdy pioneers like Dan Cruickshank in Elder Street, or the stockbroker Eric Elstob and his Argentinian artist friend Ricardo Cinalli in Fournier Street.

Although Spitalfields Market belonged to the City Corporation and the area was less than five minutes' walk from Liverpool Street and Bishopsgate and all the glare of riches, the area was situated over an invisible border in the London Borough of Tower Hamlets, then run by one of a cartel of incompetent, doctrinaire, Labour councils whose educational, town-planning, social and economic policies kept generations of inner city Britons in conditions of backward poverty, ignorance and misery for decades after the Second World War. Many local authorities connived at continued dependency and failure, as they preferred having downtrodden clients rather than an effective mixed urban population. Even a small smattering of educated, articulate residents was anathema to them as such people might be more difficult to control and bully; they might introduce unacceptable pluralist views. So, many 1960s/1970s councils actively discouraged the restoration of Georgian urban areas as they did not wish them to be taken on by people who might not vote for them, a gerrymandering policy also pursued at that time by neighbouring London boroughs like Hackney and Camden which let listed houses rot rather than sell them for rehabilitation. Outside London was even worse and Liverpool systematically destroyed two thirds of its Georgian 'West End'.

In the case of Spitalfields the regeneration and restoration of the area began in the 1970s with an influx of entrepreneurial immigrants from Bengal who started businesses and filled Brick Lane with 'Indian restaurants', and a group of dedicated architectural preservationists who tackled the historic urban fabric. I was closer to the aesthetes, though I worked as a bureaucrat with the immigrant Muslim inhabitants on the conversion into a Mosque and repair of the Huguenot Chapel, later Synagogue, an historically satisfying means of providing it with continued life. We frequented the new restaurants in Brick Lane. Once with Gavin Stamp and Dan Cruickshank, Bryan Guinness and Penelope Betjeman accompanied us to the best after a lecture by her. She addressed the proprietors in various languages, Urdu, Hindi, or in Bengali (the provincial language adopted by Bangladesh after its break away from Pakistan), or even Sylheti, but they didn't respond and she noted crisply. 'They don't even understand their own languages.' I relished the incomprehension between the daughter of the Imperial Commander-in-Chief and barely literate peasants from the tea growing terraces of Sylhet in Assam.

Spitalfields had been developed by Huguenot silk weavers from France after Louis XIV's 1685 Revocation of the Edict of Nantes and the end of toleration for Protestants. This French own goal proved one of the great boosts to the English post-Restoration economy as the Huguenots were skilled, civilized and prosperous. Those who settled in Spitalfields were silk manufacturers. They built fine houses for themselves with weavers' lofts in the attics. In the 19th century like all hand loom weavers they were gradually made redundant by the factory system and large-scale machine production.

They were succeeded by waves of poor immigrants, especially Irish then Ashkenazi Jews from Russia and central Europe, victims of the Tsarist pogroms in the 1880s and 1890s. The Ashkenazi, too, were clever and entrepreneurial and some flourished. The Huguenot Chapel at the end of Fournier Street became their synagogue but retained all its Georgian fittings and joinery, including galleries and box pews. They left the area during the blitz and moved north to Stamford Hill and the suburbs. They did not come back after the War and the bomb pocked streets declined further, threatened by misguided slum clearance and expansion of the market, the old houses divided into multiple sweatshops. Some of the freehold property was bought up by a seemingly Dickensian local firm of estate agents, Tarn & Tarn, set up in 1955 with the long-term hope of 'comprehensive redevelopment'. But in fact they proved one of the saviours of the area, as when the Spitalfields Trust was founded, with the aim of preserving the Georgian fabric, Tarn & Tarn were able to sell many of the listed houses via the Trust to people willing to buy and restore them, and subsequently they marketed the area as desirable residential.

Spitalfields contained the largest group of early-18th century houses in London and had been 'discovered' by advanced cognoscenti and aesthetes before the War as part of the general 20th century Georgian revival in English culture. Intrepid explorers ventured into the alleys, lanes and streets east of Liverpool Street and were rewarded by splendid architectural discoveries. Sacheverell Sitwell, fresh from Baroque Sicily, conjured the wonder and excitement in *British Architects and Craftsmen* (1944) of the pursuit of a remarkable old shop front dating from the reign of George II. 'And here we have it, in Artillery Lane, Spitalfields a long winding thoroughfare, so narrow that a motor cannot drive down its length, which turns and turns again, and takes us by decrepit houses and a synagogue, until we cannot think the old shop we have come this distance to see is still standing. But here it is ... double bay windows, and the wooden engaged columns at corners and on either side of the doorway in the middle. The old panes of glass are still in the windows ... It is a peculiar sensation to find this old relic in that poor and dingy street.' Upstairs in the accommodation of a Jewish school-cap maker and a poor widow, Mrs Seager, he encountered rococo panelling, high Palladian doors, a magnificent dado and a Venetian window. Sitwell fantasized that he had discovered a relic of Pompei or Herculaneum: 'this old house in Artillery Lane is as dead as though it had been covered with the lava stream. The sensation of looking at it is that of gazing upon the face of a dead person. By what miracle had it lasted through the demolitions and the German bombs? It is still inhabited, as are some of the rockcut tombs of antiquity.'

In 1974 Spitalfields still had this remote, ancient, decrepit romance, though threatened by the City Corporation who wished to expand the fruit and vegetable market, and by property developers, like British Land who saw the decaying Georgian remains as ripe for replacement with large-scale concrete, steel and glass commercial office blocks. In the face of this projected assault, we set out to save the remaining historic fabric and bring it to life again.

I came to Spitalfields via my new job with the London Historic Buildings Division, which started on 27 January 1974. The HB Division (a reactionary cell embedded in the Marxist GLC Architects' Department) was determined to revive the Georgian streets of Spitalfields. Founded in the 1890s by C.R. Ashbee, the Historic Buildings Committee had long been in the vanguard of civilised preservation in London and as early as 1908 had made a

Flier for exhibition of the travelling exhibition celebrating the preservation work of the GLC Historic Buildings Division, 1975.

Greater London Council

Conservation and Restoration

An exhibition of the work
of the Council's Historic Buildings Board

European Architectural Heritage Year 1975

photographic record of Spital Square before its demolition for the market by the City Corporation, and in 1957 it had published the admirable *Survey of London* volume devoted to the parish, with photographs, plans, measured drawings and a scholarly history of the buildings which were listed as a result. This was a key step in drawing attention, and protecting the silk weavers' houses from demolition and redevelopment. The GLC initiated a grant scheme in 1975 to assist owners willing to take on and repair the houses. Several forces came together at the same time: the GLC grant system and a handful of campaigning architects and conservationists, and The Spitalfields Trust was set up as a charity in 1977.

The Trust acquired derelict structures which were passed on to individuals able to revive them. The Spitalfields Trust has always been defiantly non-bureaucratic and highly successful as a result. It started out as it meant to go on with high profile campaigning; namely the siege of Elder Street, where a counter-revolution was organised to stop British Land who had started demolishing Nos. 5 and 7, with a high profile sit-in attracting much front-page publicity. For instance, the squatters accompanied by the Poet Laureate John Betjeman, held a dinner party in the street outside the half-deconstructed wrecks with a long table bedecked with candelabra. These tactics owed much to the example of Mariga Guinness who later bought a house nearby after her separation from Desmond Guinness.

Mariga had pioneered the elegant guerrilla tactics against vandals in the comparable Georgian slums of North Dublin after the re-foundation of the Irish Georgian Society. She had repaired a house in Mountjoy Square saved from the swing of the demolition ball, though its neighbours were destroyed, leaving hers in proud, propped isolation. Friends of hers like Mark Girouard, with his Anglo-Irish connection joined forces with Dan Cruickshank and Colin Amery from the *Architectural Press* and Marcus Binney from *Country Life,* to do the same in Spitalfields.

Dan had first visited Spitalfields in 1969, as a student recording the decaying architecture in poignant photos. He bought a house at No. 15 Elder Street before his marriage to Vickie Mills in 1981. In the end Vickie could not stand the cold and discomfort, but Dan is still in residence. No. 15 had been abandoned for over 10 years when he bought it and began its slow revival. Trailing there with Gavin Stamp, who like Dan and Colin, I met at the *Architectural Review* in Queen Anne's Gate, after coming to work in London. We would stop in the Market on the way to Indian curry suppers, to collect broken crates for stoking the fire on arrival. The resultant blaze was small mitigation for the draughty floor boards and rattling, ill-fitting sashes with cracked panes in a miraculously preserved array of old Crown glass. The rooms had wonky floors and half-finished building works in the early stages of progress towards present perfection, but all was gloriously atmospheric, lit by candles, furnished with high backed Carolean chairs, old Spitalfields silk fabrics, militaria and battered relics from forgotten colonial campaigns and imperial adventures: redcoats and sabretaches and steel helmets. Preservation battles were hatched and planned there, in the spirit of Dan's *Boys' Own* dream skirmishes.

Gavin and my meeting with Dan and Colin at the *Architectural Review* had an equally picturesque backdrop, the *Bride of Denmark* in the basement of the 'ArchiRev' in Queen Anne's Gate, Westminster. Dan edited the 'Astragal' column in the *Architects Journal* to which we provided occasional conservation titbits and campaigning pieces, while Colin Amery was the deputy editor of the *Architectural Review*, the journal's smarter, glossier, more arty stable-mate to which I provided the occasional academic article on the Wyatts or Georgian model farms or indeed Christ Church Spitalfields. Colin was charming and wrote beautifully himself, but was rather episodic as an editor, being 'up and down' and sometimes off for days suffering pangs of depression. (He was 'let go' in 1979, becoming the architectural writer for the *Financial Times* and adviser to Sainsbury's.) He was a north London boy—his family having owned a business in the City—but after Southgate Grammar School and a good degree from Sussex University he became a tenant of the Girouard family in Notting Hill, and shared some of Mark Girouard's architectural enthusiasms, combining a passion for historic buildings with hero-worship of the uncompromising Modern architect Denys Lasdun, then designing the National Theatre on the South Bank. (I was later one of Colin's godparents, with Blanche Girouard, when he was received into the Catholic Church).

The 'Bride' was an evening meeting place for architectural enthusiasts, a sort of club, as the bar was opened after office hours, and the staff, contributors and visitors would congregate down there in its warm retrospective environs. It had been created in 1947 from bits of demolished Victorian pubs and bomb sites by the legendary editor de Cronin Hastings, John Betjeman and fellow spirits like Ian Nairn and Gordon Cullen. It was a precocious example of revived Victorian enthusiasm. It had old looking-glass etched with gloriously florid gilt lettering advertising Bass ales, and well stocked shelves with serried bottles and barrels. There was a mahogany bar, padded benches and tall stools. There was even a stuffed (half) lion in a glass case staring fiercely through dried tropical grasses (rescued by Pevsner who presented it), a large turtle shell, and not least a mirror signed by famous past guests including Frank Lloyd Wright. The ceiling was cunningly 'smoked' to look like a real Victorian pub. Of course, when the Architectural Press ceased to be a family firm and was taken over by standard bureaucratic corporationism, the building was sold and the developer ripped it all out. I wonder where the lion went?

At least their type was fended off in Spitalfields, and one by one the decrepit wrecks were acquired and nursed back to life. In Fournier Street, the pioneers were the painters Gilbert and George. They used to eat in the Market Caff every day and glare at passers-by. A nearby house was acquired by Penny d'Erlanger (descendant of one of the founders of the Georgian Group, Baroness d'Erlanger), who employed the architect Philip Jebb to restore it beautifully, but she found the area too raw, and understandably moved back to Kensington. A deceased architect from

Bath, whose name I've forgotten, bought no. 14, next door to Gilbert and George, but sold it on to Eric Elstob who carried out a somewhat do-it-yourself restoration (he stripped the paint from the panelling, seen by some Spitalfielders as a solecism) and introduced murals by Ricardo Cinalli who specialises in vast baroque mythological nudes with a touch of Salvador Dali. They included the ceiling of the staircase where a huge naked Greek god sprawled seemingly dangling, frontally over the space. As Gavin remarked, anyone who glanced up unawares was in for a shock!

Ricardo remembered when he first arrived in London in 1973, meeting and being taken to see the house in Fournier Street which Eric was buying. 'We came to Spitalfields on a very depressing day. My God it was a dump! I said to Eric, "Are you crazy?" It was overwhelming, the rats, the prostitutes, and meths drinkers outside the house. And the minute he opened the door I could see the place was in horrible condition. But Eric explained to me the history of the Huguenots, and the bells in the church rang and suddenly I understood the magic. He said to me, "You are invited to join my life's project to restore this house."' Ricardo said 'Yes', and was with Eric until his death. He still lives in Spitalfields today but in another house in Puma Court, where he continues to paint in a studio with a skylight framing the majestic Baroque spire of Christ Church.

They took seven years to repair No. 14, doing much of the work themselves, for as Ricardo said, they had no money in those days, though Eric made some later as a stockbroker at de Zoete & Bevan in the City. Decades later, following Eric's memorial service in the City, we all went back to Fournier Street for the Wake, and gloriously the fully restored complete change of bells rang from the tower of Christ Church in his memory. I went into the splendid, by then fully re-created Hawksmoor interior and stood alone in the magnificent Roman nave, listening to the bells ringing so triumphantly, an elegiac moment.

I was more closely involved in the early stages of the resurrection of the church than the houses. We founded the Friends of Christ Church Spitalfields in 1976 and Eric was our treasurer, and then the chairman. When he died, he left money towards the restoration. My strongest early impression of the parish was of Hawksmoor's baroque masterpiece rising sublime, majestic, heroic above the slums. I had seen its spire out of the windows of trains to East Anglia from Liverpool Street, but nothing prepares you for the architectural shock of seeing it on the ground. After winding like Sitwell through Artillery Lane, past that shop front, and a brick double house which I regrettably encouraged the developer to paint (a mistake) and there—bang-across Commercial Road—it rises in all its idiosyncratic Baroque glory. In 1974 it was as decayed as its surroundings, but in my imagination it appeared as a poignant contrast, restored and magnificently maintained; its stonework gleaming white, its interior radiant with gilding and polished oak, 18th century organ voluntaries thundering beneath the rich Corinthian capitals and noble panelled stucco ceiling. We wanted it to be a landmark of spiritual achievement and transcendent genius amidst the ruined depressed lives and filthy crumbling houses. Now, of course, it is, but presides over a *quartier* inhabited by prosperous fund managers and minimalist BBC executives rather than the first-wave conservation heroes, let alone the poor. Is it the tragedy of London that prosperity destroys the spirit?

The Friends of Christ Church was set up under the aegis of the Historic Buildings Division with Bob Chitham (an architect who had commanded submarines) and John Earl (expert on London Theatres which owe their miraculous survival largely to him and the efforts of the Historic Buildings Committee), with local pioneers and chaps from Save, the campaigning force which had been founded in 1975, European Conservation Year. Several of us attended the opening meeting of Save, sitting on the floor in John Harris's elegant neo-Classical octagonal office at the RIBA Drawings Collection in Portman Square (now part of the yuppy Home House club). Save helped in particular with the opening concert at Christ Church intended as the first shot in the war. A key figure was an HB colleague and contemporary Jonathan Balkind

Jonathan Balkind. Secretary of the Friends of Christ Church, Spitalfields and JMR's colleague in the Historic Buildings Division.

who acted as the Secretary of the Friends, and as the musical impresario who organized a succession of concerts of unexpected ambition which grew into the Spitalfields Festival.

Jonathan joined the HB Division at the same time as me and become one of my closest friends and allies. He was the most extraordinary person. Born in Los Angeles of South African Jewish parents, he was the stepson of Sydney Brenner CH, the Cambridge Nobel Prize winning biologist (an expert on the Genetics of the worm *caenor habditis elegans*), Fellow of Kings, and founder of the Molecular Sciences Institute in Berkeley, California. Jonathan had started reading medicine at Kings, but had been thrown out for heinous offences—it was rumoured for having carried out an illegal abortion on a girlfriend, or stabbing someone, or having a gun in his room, possibly all three. He then studied architecture at the Architectural Association in Bedford Square. He didn't finish that course either and decided to go into property, doing up a thatched cottage in Suffolk, selling it for a profit, and then buying a house in Chalcot Road, 'Belsizia', which he converted into three flats with his own large penthouse on top, enjoying views over Primrose Hill, and a tiny kitchen from which he produced Lucullan feasts in a cylindrical space (or was that the bathroom? Anyway, it was very small.) The flat was all geometry and strong primary colours—reds and blues and greens—of a Post-Modernist type popularized at Cambridge by John Outram. It gave Jonathan much scope to demonstrate his distinctive brand of quirky individualism, as well as cooking delicious dinners and entertaining his friends to Tosca and Don Carlos and recherché bassoon pieces from his enormous collection of disc gramophone records. He was caught by one of the Heath economic crashes in the early '70s and saved from bankruptcy by his mother who bailed him out. He lived at Chalcot Road for the rest of his life and it was a regular berth for me in the '70s and the early '80s, just down the hill from where I lived then in Heath Street, Hampstead.

He needed a job in 1974, so joined the Historic Buildings Division. Never can such an unlikely character have worked in a public body. It says much for his employers and colleagues that they recognised the talents embedded in the uncontrollable, acerbic, bolshy eccentric and used them. They unleashed him on Spitalfields! There he ran the grant programme and took over Christ Church with spectacular if financially incontinent results.

I can see that he must have been a 'difficult child'. At the Perse School in Cambridge, he played rugby where he gave a classic demonstration of his peculiar brand of illogical logic. Sent off the pitch by a master for some misdemeanour or other, he climbed on to the cross bar of the goal posts and refused to come down. As dusk approached, the master's commands softened into beseeching requests of increasing meekness. Jonathan's response was 'your sending me off was unreasonable, so I am responding by acting in an equally unreasonable way. I am staying here until you apologise.' The reader will be left to guess who blinked first. It played a part that he was big and burly and very strong with curly black hair. He could park his car in a crowded street in Soho by lifting it physically into a tiny slot too narrow to drive into. At work it was like sitting at a desk next to the Farnese Hercules in a jersey.

I can see now that he set out to befriend (seduce?) me, but I suppose I was naïve at the time. I was twenty-five when we met but had inherited the views of an older generation, and found it extraordinary, and exciting, when on visiting his family in Cambridge, Sydney and May (his mother, a psychiatrist) put us into the same room without a blink, treating us as a couple. I have always had a slight crush on rugger players, a product of my education with the 'rugby macs' at one of 'those sinister Scotch academies in the Arctic Circle', but he was not my type and at first I thought him dull, tiresome and 'difficult'. I was right about the last. Gradually, I found his conversation fascinating and often sympathetic. There was a particular occasion in the office I remember vividly when he was talking about the Roman aristocracy as one did, of course, over the buff files and grey metal furniture in the attic hideaway of the HB division in County Hall, looking out through dormers over the giant lion to the Palace of Westminster. He knew all about the Doria, the Massimi, and the Colonna. It turned out he had a friend Felicity Bowes-Lyon (Mason) who had a flat in Rome (and one on the Île in Paris, and one in New York, and one in London) where he stayed regularly. He started using the term 'we'; was he referring to his own very complicated and changeable ménage, or me? I wasn't sure. The experience made me realise that Life is a great deal more complicated and difficult than one might like.

At home in Cambridge he introduced me to fascinating people whom he knew: Peter Bicknell of the School of Architecture at Grecian Downing, Michael Jaffé the art historian, and Peter Avery at Gothic Kings. Peter was the archetype of the urbane don, much more polished than the slightly sub fusc specimens of the genus one was used to at St Andrews or Oxford. He was an expert on Persian poetry, a top ratchet snob, and a kinsman of the Chetwynd-Talbots of Ingestre in Staffordshire, regaling me at length about Pugin's Alton towers (described by Pevsner as the 'apotheosis of Catholic Romanticism'), when he realised I was interested in architecture.

There were flashing warnings, though, in Jonathan's immediate family. His half-siblings had his strong individualism but manifested in even more unconventional, out of control, destructive and altogether less creative forms. His sister ended up as a registered heroin addict. I felt the things we had in common were thin ice over vertiginous, unknowable differences, yet he was clever, gentle, and generous to me. The unconventional, cosmopolitan, otherness was liberating and to some extent our characters were complementary. For a time I rather fell for him and it transformed my attitude to my work for the Historic Buildings Committee. County Hall became for me what his prison cell in the Citadel of Parma was to Fabrizio when it seemed to contain everything in the world that was dear to him. Or so it seemed for a few months from 1974 to 1976, but later I left him to his serious relationships, with a married plumber and an alcoholic bassoonist of genius.

Christ Church was one of the 'fifty new churches' established by Act of Parliament in 1711, when Queen Anne's Tory government used the coal tax to erect additional Anglican parishes in the expanding suburbs of London. In the event only twelve churches were built, all of them masterpieces of English baroque. Their grandeur demonstrated the position of the Church of England in the Stuart-supporting Tories' vision of Britain. The Commissioners of the new churches were Wren, Vanbrugh and Thomas Archer. Under them were two surveyors, one of whom was Nicholas Hawksmoor of the Office of Works who designed six of the new churches himself, including Christ Church which displays all his idiosyncratic grandeur. The west front is a knock-out composition of three superimposed Serlian triumphal arches topped by an obelisk 202 feet high. The interior is dominated by giant arcades of Corinthian columns, grandest of the Classical Orders, and at the East end is a regal Venetian window. The royal character was emphasized in the early-19th century when a huge Coade Stone trophy of the Hanoverian Royal Arms was set up on the chancel beam. Originally there were galleries along the side aisles supported on carved oak brackets and the lower windows were in two arcaded tiers creating an effect like a Roman aqueduct along Fournier Street. Alterations by Ewan Christian in 1850 removed the galleries (and stacked them at the west end like the tiered boxes in an opera house) and lengthened the aisle windows substituting more the effect of a dreary non-conformist chapel than Hawksmoor's staccato Baroque genius.

The church was in poor condition at the end of the War and the roof close to collapse. The parish transferred to the Church Hall in Hanbury Street in 1960 leaving Christ Church derelict and with an unsafe notice served on it. Demolition was threatened. Disaster was averted by the Bishop of Stepney, the saintly Trevor Huddleston who ensured that the Church Commissioners used the money from the sale of St John's Smith Square for a concert hall to rebuild the roof. That kept the structure safe. The living at Christ Church was in the hands of a Victorian Evangelical Trust which had acquired a member of East End benefices to keep them 'low church' in the face of successful Victorian Anglo-Catholic missionary activity under a succession of Tractarian Bishops of London.

Perhaps not as enthusiastic about Baroque architecture as some people, successive rectors of Christ Church nevertheless cared about the people of the parish and in the 1960s a rehabilitation centre for homeless alcoholic men, under the patronage of Princess Alexandra, was established in the crypt which kept part of the building in use. The derelict nave filled up with stored rubbish, birds flying in and out through broken window panes, the marble monuments encased in plywood coverings.

The Friends immediately established good relations with the Rector, Eddie Stride, who made it clear he would move back in and hold services in the church if it were restored, so long as the building work could be funded from outside bodies and not from the parish's own limited resources. That became the aim and William

Whitfield was appointed the architect with his assistant 'Red' Mason who painstakingly researched the history of the fabric with the intention of reinstating the side galleries and the whole interior to Hawksmoor's design. The Friends first task, proving their serious intent, was to clear out, clean the interior and reinstate the side aisle windows to two tiers, reversing Ewan Christian's unfortunate alteration. Their other early achievement was the establishment of the concerts and music festival to show the potential for wider cultural use and to attract attention and funds. The work was done in phases. Railings and Purbeck paving were restored at the west end, the parish room in the tower refurbished, and the portico roof renewed. The crypt was cleared of burials in 1984-6 using archaeologists and social anthropologists, which revealed much new historical information about the 18th and 19th century inhabitants of the East End published in a two volume study.

When the portico and forecourt were repaired they were arranged with the railings reinstated to the original design, but with a special indent for the tea van to prevent it being gentrified away. It had parked there every night to minister to tramps since the War. The parish moved back into the restored shell of the church, holding all their services there in 1987. That marked victory. Cleaning and repairs to the exterior stonework continued in the 1990s. Full scale restoration of the interior was finally achieved between 2002 and 2004 with grants from the Heritage Lottery Fund, English Heritage and Simon Sainsbury. The galleries were reinstated, the organ restored with gilt mitres and crowns on top, and the original stone colour, off-white and gilt decoration revived.

Our role twenty-six years earlier had been to start the project rolling, introduce hope, plan a long-term strategy, encourage the rector and parish and obtain wider support, ready for the heavy-lifters to take over later. 'Red' Mason was involved as architect all the way through and after William Whitfield retired in 2000, he transferred to Purcell Miller Tritton who completed the interior work. Thus the most complex and sumptuous of Hawksmoor's

London church interiors, as well as his extraordinarily original exterior, can now be enjoyed once more as a work of art of international significance, and a living protestant church; so the major monument of Spitalfields presides in all its architectural glory and in full Christian use once more.

The Friends of Christ Church Spitalfields was established in November 1976 at a consultation on the future of the church with a musical recital to demonstrate the acoustics held by invitation of the rector under the auspices of Save led by Marcus Binney. About two hundred people crowded into the church and heard a concert given by the Renaissance Singers and the Hertfordshire Chamber Orchestra; it was the modest overture to a series of increasingly ambitious concerts held there in the years to come. The centre of the nave had been cleared specially for the occasion. A group worked over the previous days moving decades of accumulated rubbish. We took it out into the churchyard to the south and burnt it all on huge bonfires, a satisfying task.

The tramps' tea van was a most welcome resource, steaming mugs of strong black brew helping to ameliorate the November cold, much more intense inside than out, as is always the case with damp, disused, derelict, old buildings. There were no pews nor even a proper floor, just the brick top of the crypt vault. Seating was obtained from the nearby public swimming baths in Ironmonger Row which for some reason had a large stock of 1960s tubular steel chairs. I never knew whether this loan was authorised by anyone in the council, or whether it was just a grab and run raid by Jonathan in full highwayman mode. (I've always found that the best way to deal with bureaucracy is never to ask but just to go ahead and 'do a Copenhagen'.)

After the concert, which was a success as the audience turned up coated, gloved and scarved, and provided good business for the tea van during the interval, it was agreed to found a charitable trust. This was instituted immediately as the Friends of Christ Church (or as immediately as the lawyers could manage it) and the trustees were all the usual suspects, Gavin and Colin, Eric and Marcus, me, and Sophie Andreae who had just come to work for Save on coming down from Cambridge, as well as a strong GLC contingent including Louis Bondi, Chairman of the Historic Buildings Committee. There were also distinguished older luminaries from the wider world who agreed to be trustees, notably Denys Lasdun who had a great enthusiasm for Hawksmoor, and Liz Kennet whose husband Wayland had successfully promoted the Civic Amenities Act in 1968 which made the historic buildings laws in England effective for the first time. Working in Harold Wilson's government, he was in my view, apart from Michael Heseltine (who saved what remained of Liverpool), the most effective government conservationist of the post-War era. There has been no one like them since. The older trustees' contribution to Christ Church added maturity and established clout to the enthusiasm of youngsters like us. Nicholas Serota, who was then director of the Whitechapel Art Gallery, was also a Hawksmoor enthusiast and helped mount an exhibition in the church on its history and proposals for restoration and to publish a compendium of historical essays in 1979 for the 250th anniversary of the church.

The Rectory of Christ Church where the Reverend Eddy Stride lived was next door at No. 2 Fournier Street, a splendid 18th century panelled house and beyond it at No. 4 was an even more splendid house with a solid mahogany staircase, unique in London and only paralleled at Houghton. It had been acquired via the Spitalfields Trust for £20,000 and was being restored by Michael Gillingham and Donald Findlay of the *Scotsman* newspaper family (who gave the Scottish National Portrait Gallery to Edinburgh), using Julian Harrap as their architect. Michael was a rotund man of several specialisms. Having read law at Cambridge, he earned his living as an expert connoisseur dealing in Chinese porcelain, jade and Asian works of art, first at Spinks then at Sparks—hence my nickname for him 'Spinkerysparkery'—but his strongest interest was in historic church organs of which he was the leading expert in the country, advising Noel Mander on restoration of many important instruments including those at St James, Clerkenwell, Chichester

Cathedral, and St Lawrence, Appleby-in-Westmorland. He was especially interested in the rare 18th century organ at Christ Church which dated from 1733, and was the largest in England when built, and conceived the plans for its restoration as it had not worked for half a century.

Meetings of the Friends Trust in due course tended to take place at Michael and Donald's after it was repaired as it was more comfortable and beautifully furnished than the Rectory and Michael, who liked cooking, often provided a supper. He in due course became chairman of the Friends for a time. No. 4 Fournier Street, and Michael and Donald's hospitality, became a regular destination for me, and I went there for supper and gossip every Sunday evening when I was in London and had not gone away for the weekend. When he died of cancer, aged 40, Donald left me the Egremont-made grandfather clock from his sitting room in Fournier Street.

Two of the most memorable concerts were productions of Handel's *Israel in Egypt* (1739) and Gluck's *Armide* (1777). They were both produced by Richard Hicox whom Jonathan introduced to Spitalfields and who became musical director of the Festival. The performance of *Israel in Egypt* in April 1977 was one of the proudest moments of my life, sitting in the Piranesian grandeur of the derelict church which we had cleared with our own sweat, where many of the window panes were still broken, as the stupendous sounds of Handel's oratorio swelled to fill the architecture, anticipating revival, resurrection and new life. The platforms, timpani, harpsichords and temporary overhead lighting were all hired by the Friends for the occasion. Richard Hicox, the leader of the 'authentic' movement in music, gave his services free, and brought his own singers and orchestra. These were complemented by two chamber choirs to make over a hundred voices, and six soloists. The splendid music with trumpets and drums and three choirs echoing round the ruined baroque interior was deeply moving. It proved that the acoustics were perfect for Handel.

Jonathan, Eric Elstob, Christopher Andreae (Sophie's youngest brother) and I slaved all the week before to clean up the place ready for the concert. This involved removing *six tons* of waste paper from the nave, sacks of rotten potatoes from the porch, masses of worm eaten woodwork, old mattresses, and other filth and junk. On the Saturday afternoon before the evening concert we weeded the portico and front steps and washed the marble memorial tablets in the vestibule, our efforts assisted by innumerable local children who just emerged and lent a hand, attracted by the bonfire and our cheerful demeanour. A photo of us sweeping the church floor appeared in the *Times*, on the social page next to the Court circular, and the *Guardian* published a piece regretting the all-pervasive 'smell of cats' (actually tramps!) rather than celebrating the architecture: no vision, no romance, no soul.

Before the concert Michael Gillingham organised a buffet supper in the nave, part supplied by Marks & Spencer and various local suppliers (no shortage of fruit and veg). It struck me as a characteristically English occasion: picnicking in a derelict church in a slum. I couldn't see educated French or Germans doing it. It was second nature to the architectural apparatchiks, but even the musical grandees led by George Harewood who had come specially for the Oratorio entered into the spirit of the occasion and 'enjoyed it'.

Armide in 1982 was an even more spectacular occasion. Jonathan somehow enticed 'Woomie' Wagner from Bayreuth to design the production. Felicity Palmer (as the Sorceress) and Anthony Rolfe Johnson (as the Christian Knight) sang the leads and gave what seemed to us an electric performance though a later generation have found it too Brahms-like and over dramatic. Though a glorious *tour de force, Armide* did not make a profit, unlike *Israel,* and in fact it lost £20,000.

In due course the festival, as it had become, was sloughed off to a more professional set-up, independent of the restoration programme and fund raising. Looking back, I am still astonished by the ambition, scale and grandeur of the musical events which were put on. So was the rector, who taking advantage of the clean and now lit if still somewhat derelict church—at least the windows were re-glazed as our prime repair job—held the first service there for nearly thirty years, which we felt was encomium enough.

As the 1970s became the 1980s, some of us centred more on Bloomsbury. Following Gavin Stamp's marriage in 1982 to Alexandra Artley whom he had met at the 'Bride of Denmark', for she too worked at the Architectural Press, they bought a former lodging house dating from *circa* 1820 in St Chad Street, off Argyle Square, near Kings Cross Station, which they restored as their house, stripping 50 layers of nicotine-impregnated wallpaper from the walls. It had lost its original chimney-pieces and Dan and I each gave the happy couple a marble chimney-piece of the appropriate Regency reeded and roundel design for the principal rooms. Mine had been rescued from the Old Rectory at Egham when that was demolished. Our chimney-pieces are still there in St Chad Street and presumably protected by the listing, though the Stamps themselves sold the house and moved on thirty years ago.

There were differences in Bloomsbury. Their house was early-19th century rather than early-18th century. There were more prostitutes in the streets than alcoholic tramps. The prostitutes had a long history; there were already complaints about them in 1827 and what were called 'hotels' in the 19th century were brothels. On Booth's Poverty Map in 1889, the neighbourhood of Kings Cross was coloured black and blue for 'semi-criminal' and 'chronic want'. That still applied in the 1980s.

One of the big changes from crate-strewn Spitalfields was that there were now coal fires rather than wood. There was a coal cellar under the pavement, still with its circular cast iron lid or *operculum* (as Dan called it) in the pavement, and Gavin somehow found an old-fashioned coal merchant who used to shoot hessian sacks of coal into the underworld with a happy rumbling crash such as must have been an everyday sound in Victorian London.

Jolly evenings were spent in the first floor drawing room with its maculated walls—the Stamps never got beyond the stripped plaster—hung with architectural engravings, sitting in front of a

Gavin Stamp, wearing the military coat bought in Kirkby Lonsdale, which his daughters did not approve.

hot coal fire, and drinking red plonk and eating home delivered pizza from 'round the corner'.

Regular habitués were Jonathan Meades, general architectural pundit, and Jonathan Glancey, architectural critic of the *Guardian*, or Fr Anthony Symdonson then an Anglo-Catholic clergyman who married Alex and Gavin in Holy Cross, Cromer Street, the neighbouring High Church, and later converted to Catholicism, going the whole hog and becoming a Jesuit priest. He was the leading expert and eventually wrote a book on Sir Ninian Comper,

Betjeman's hero and last of the great British Gothic Revival architects, whereas Gavin's special scholarly subject (on which he had written his Cambridge PhD) was George Gilbert Scott (architect of Norwich Catholic Cathedral) and his third son, Sir Giles Gilbert Scott O.M. (of Liverpool Anglican Cathedral).

Anthony and Gavin as a result were closely involved with Watts & Co, the ecclesiastical vestment-makers situated in a crypt in Tufton Street behind Westminster Abbey which perpetuated the designs of the great Victorians, Pugin and Scott, Bodley and Comper. It now belonged to Sir Giles Gilbert Scott's grand-daughter Elizabeth married to a Hoare of the Bank which helped. Gavin and Anthony helped write Watts' history, brochures and sales publicity. The name had been chosen in 1874 by George Gilbert Scott Jnr. and G.F. Bodley because 'What's in a name?' This connection introduced a strong streak of Victorian ecclesiology into the conversation at St Chad Street.

Despite his clerical calling, Anthony had an acidulous tongue and was a master of sarcasm and mimicry. A particular target was modern Anglican kitsch, especially the 'vestments' and ridiculous, badly-proportioned mitres gradually assumed by Archbishops of Canterbury in the course of the 20th century. Anglican Bishops, although incorporating mitres as opposed to crests in their arms, never wore such Romish trappings in the heyday of the National Church. As a fashion statement in their decline, now they did. Why, expostulated Anthony, were such vestments always in resolutely non-liturgical colours such as turquoise and 'Tango Orange', why the ubiquitous cliché of embroidered flames? 'Very *symbolic*, I suppose. Symbolic of *WHAT*...?'

Worst of all, in his eyes, were the ubiquitous School of Beryl Dean altar frontals which he saw as public demonstrations of sub-Expressionist bad taste, a kind of English lower middle class female folk art, to be discouraged. He mimicked their creation by 'dewy-eyed' women dressed in 'fuchsia pink trouser suits', stitching and sewing, embroidering and batiking and needling away, to produce the incongruous horrors that detract from every medieval cathedral and major church in the country with the honourable exception of the Royal Peculiars of St George's Chapel, Windsor, and Westminster Abbey. Those still display well-designed historic needlework in correct liturgical colours by Gilbert Scott and Ninian Comper.

The ecclesiology was ameliorated by the more political contribution of Meades and Glancey. The former, in particular, was horrified by Mrs Thatcher's policies then gathering full traction. Personally, I was in favour of a bit of union bashing and had little sympathy for the south Yorkshire miners where my father's cousin John Cotton was the Circuit Judge and had to try the Orgreave rioters and their violent chums. The Derbyshire and Nottinghamshire miners were altogether a better bunch, and their subsequent betrayal and the closure of their relatively modern mines still rankles. Despite a bit of Tory-Lefty difference and full blooded debate, we were all agreed and deeply sceptical about the 'privatisation' policy which merely transformed incompetent nationalised industries into irresponsible, unaccountable corporate monopolies, locked into passé management systems derived from failed 1960s Harvard Business School nostrums. This became one of Gavin's strongest beliefs and the chief strand of Jonathan Meades' eulogy at Gavin's funeral service thirty years later.

Alex had a genuine social conscience enhanced by her encounters in the streets of St Pancras, pushing the prams of their two baby daughters Agnes and Cecilia, whose names recalled the Stamps' honeymoon in Rome. She expressed her views in regular articles in the *Spectator* until worry about the horrors of the Underclass eventually unbalanced her mind. In the early happy days at St Chad Street, she was writing in a lighter social comedy mood. She transferred from the *Architectural Press* to *Harpers & Queen*, which had a modern open plan office in Soho, open-plan except for Betty Kenward, the legendary social diarist who occupied an enclosure embosomed in lace curtains and vases of cut flowers where she dictated in her archaic clipped tones lists of whom she had met at Lady so-and-so's little party in Chelsea to a succession of skivvies, gals from good families who on the whole did not last long. They might have had to be 'let go' because they had pronounced Cundit Street Conduit, or expressed a liking for 'common' vegetables like carrots. The editor was a middle-aged valetudinarian Italian who traipsed around the office swathed in shawls, but the driving force was Anne Barr, creator of the 'Sloane Ranger'. It was her humorous social vision that inspired Alex.

She and I would sit on the floor in front of the coal fire in St Chad Street, knocking back the plonk and composing what we thought were hysterically funny articles under pseudonyms John Seymour Smith, Jan van Oik, or William Dibdin. It was as the latter that I wrote a piece on Raine Spencer's rape of the art collection at Althorp. Raine had been chairman of the GLC Historic Buildings Committee and was a large force in saving Covent Garden threatened by bulldozing for a 6-lane urban motorway to bypass Strand, so she had her good points, but she was completely uneducated and a ridiculous figure in her crinolines and swept up hair, like those dolls the Hyacinth Bucket-type of New Yorkers use to hide their telephones or lavatory brushes. I enjoyed the story that she broke off an engagement to Peter Coates, the garden writer, not because he was obviously gay, but because she didn't want to go through life being called Rain(e) Coat(e)s.

After Johnnie Spencer's stroke (when she devotedly nursed him back to life), she took over complete control of Althorp and systematically sold all the *seicento* religious paintings and much else from the collection through the back door to knowing dealers for a fraction of their true value. Many of the pictures had been exempted from Death Duties as being of national historic and artistic pre-eminence, but that meant nothing to her, though it did leave the family trustees with a large retrospective tax bill in due course.

Anyway, I persuaded Alex to let me do a piece publicising what I saw as a national scandal and an outrage. It was easy to do, because I discovered that the London Library catalogue of the Althorp Collection by Kenneth Garlick had been liberally annotated by an anonymous hand in pencil with 'Sold by the Harpie' against every missing art work, which enabled us to publish lists. Charles Spencer had no idea until then of the full extent of his wicked stepmother's depredations of the family heirlooms. He ordered 30 copies of the magazine.

Our favourite joint task, composed over suppers, was a conservationist joke paperback inspired by Anne Barr's *Sloane Ranger Handbook*, with caricatures of our friends called the *New Georgian Hand Book, A First Look at the Conservation Way of Life*, published in 1985. Dan Cruickshank was the inspiration for 'Pop Baroque' (he and his wife Vickie are shown on the front cover), Glynn and Carrie Boyd Harte for the 'Soanies', Gervase Jackson-Stops (of the National Trust) for 'Batchelor Folly', Stephen Calloway (Roy Strong's assistant at the V&A), for the 'Liquorice Allsorts' and the fruits of my field trips to North East London and the adjacent Cockney suburbs in the Essex Border Lands, while revising the statutory lists of historic buildings in Redbridge and Waltham Forest, for 'Kentucky Fried Georgian' (a term I invented).

Some people might find it childish, full of silly jokes, puns and *double entendres*: 'Know a man by his obelisks'. Sir Anthony Wagner, Garter, advised me to be careful about lending my name to such light-hearted nonsense as it could damage my scholarly reputation. We had a wonderful time. It was illustrated with humorous drawings by Lawrence Mynott from the Royal College of Art, then another habitué of St Chad Street before he decamped with his wife to Tangier. It was a success and has become something of a collector's item among a younger generation. An intern at Sotheby's I met the other day told me he had 50 copies as he bought them as soon as they came up on Abe or Amazon. It is the best record of our efforts in the 1970s and 1980s.

2

Young Fogeys

WORK WITH THE preservation of historic buildings in London impinged on a wider world taking in writing, journalism, politics and the purlieus of the *Spectator*. Many acquaintances and friends coalesced after coming to London, and a superficial similarity of interests—love of old houses, bicycles, tweed coats and tailored suits, educated speech and tastes—led to us being lumped together and described as a *Phenomenon*, 'Young Fogeys'. We were analysed and interviewed in the press and television about our pinstripes, High Tory views and polished brogues. If it amused people, well and good, but we were not that remarkable. Some of my contemporaries who went into the City and therefore escaped journalistic attention were even more fogey-ish than the writers and aesthetes. Men such as Michael Hodges who joined Morgan Grenfell but was more interested in historic churches than banking, or Richard Grantley who succeeded his father in the House of Lords and became briefly the only UKIP Member of Parliament, let alone the chancery barristers in panelled rooms full of red tape, or those happy souls who left London immediately to live in large houses in Derbyshire and write elegant essays on Proust and Stendhal.

Young Fogeys were just part of a continuous tradition in English life, and little different from their predecessors and successors, but they stuck out more in the 1970s and 80s for a social reason which I do not think has been mentioned in print. In earlier 20th century generations there had not been such a stark cultural divide in Britain between the privately educated and other classes. The Grammar Schools had masked and tapered differences; and knowledge of history, French or Latin and love of reading books, music and art were more widely diffused. Even at the lower end of the scale, because of Sunday School and the prominent role played by parish life in towns, suburbs and villages up to the 1960s, there was a wider cultural awareness across all classes, which derived from and reflected the sophisticated nature of the Anglican clergy.

The greatest achievement of the Church of England, was to achieve a universally educated clergy, unlike the Orthodox or Romans Catholics, and to maintain it over four centuries. When I was a child it was impossible to be further than five miles in England from someone who understood Ancient Greek, one indicator of civilisation. After the abolition of grammar schools and decline in the calibre of the clergy, those people who had been independently educated (or came from Northern Ireland) and were graduates of the older universities, became a more conspicuous minority when most of the population were products of State Comprehensives then in their untried experimental phase, largely devoid of art, music and games. Young Fogeys were not new, but in the fields of journalism, writing and the arts, where a modicum of old-fashioned literacy and knowledge then remained essential, they were suddenly more visibly different.

Alan Watkins (a columnist in the *Observer*) invented the term 'Young Fogey' as a joke in May 1984, describing the young men he saw in Fleet Street and Doughty Street. 'The young fogey is libertarian, but not liberal. He is a Conservative but has no time for Mrs Thatcher. He is a disciple of Evelyn Waugh and tends to be unsentimentally religious. He hates modern architecture, and fusses about old missals, old grammar books, syntax and punctuation. He moans over the difficulty of buying decent bread and cheddar worthy of the name. He loves to go for walks and travel by train.' Watkins cited Charles Moore, then the editor of the *Spectator* as one of the extreme examples of the species, and the Prince of Wales as their idol. The categorisation, like all clever half-truths, took off and was promoted for a brief moment in the English press, and also appended to a certain sort of Anglophile, preppy or would-be preppy American.

There is now even a site on *Wikipedia* ('Wonkipedia') which describes this non-existent socio-political phenomenon with historical solemnity: 'The movement reached its peak in the 1980s with champions such as A.N. Wilson, Gavin Stamp and John Martin Robinson and a relatively widespread following but has declined since.' Looking back after nearly forty years, it is possible to discern a certain congruence of views and style and we were certainly friends or at least known to one another, and those of us still alive remain so, but like many generalisations, the cited insignia of fogeydom did not exist. Far from having no time for Mrs Thatcher, Charles Moore has written a sympathetic three-volume official biography. Gavin Stamp was never Conservative and remained an Attlee-Welfare-State supporter throughout his life. Andrew Wilson was going through an Agnostic phase in the 1980s.

I did not disapprove of Modern Architecture; I have always been enthusiastic about all architecture and based my judgments on quality and genius rather than style as such; though obviously old buildings derive qualities from age not immediately available to a new structure, such as tone, texture, historical memory, and the charm of simply being old which gives interest even to mediocre places as demonstrated in any old street. On the other hand, new buildings can have special qualities not present in old buildings. Norman Foster's finely detailed three-dimensional geometry is only possible with computer-aided drawing (CAD), as in the impressive glazed roof over the Great Court of the British Museum.

Charles Moore (who knew what he was talking about) said that it was not a matter of sharing or affirming positive doctrines. It was more a question of what you were against: 'It is compulsory to dislike feminists, the *Guardian*, immigration, all modern church liturgies, the BBC and Edward Heath.' Beyond that there was considerable freedom. You could be homosexual, but never gay. You could commit adultery but not have an open marriage. You should be anti-anti-smoking. You could hate America or Russia. (I prefer Russia and believe we should have a Special Relationship with its neo-Tsarist government as a bulwark against the Chinese and

Islamic threats from the East. Britain and Russia are independent bulwarks on either side of Europe.) It was certainly not necessary to vote Conservative, the *Private Eye* crew never did. Nor for that matter did I ever ride a bicycle, and am not able to and have no sense of balance.

Nevertheless we were observed like specimens of Lepidoptera by an assortment of journalists with nothing else to write about. Suzanne Lowry wrote a book called the *Young Fogey Handbook* copycatting Anne Barr and Peter Yorke's clever *Sloane Ranger Handbook*. Andrew Wilson in the *Literary Review* described the hard-working journalist-author, whom I do not think any of us met, as a 'talentless hackette'. That at least must have disabused her of any belief that Young Fogeys might be chivalrous Victorian throw-backs.

Alexandra Artley (Mrs Stamp) encouraged the interest and publicity as providing fodder for her articles in *Harpers* or the *Spectator*. She described me as 'pure fogey crystals, just add claret'. Nicholas Coleridge wrote an article at her instigation in the *Evening Standard*, interviewing me in my Bloomsbury house. He himself was perhaps always a bit too glitzy to be taken as a Young Fogey, though he ticked many of the boxes.

Alex, shrewdly I now see, saw that there was parallel interest there and it might help to market our own *New Georgian Handbook*, and indeed the two works can often be found as twin, dog-eared old paperbacks on Abe, Amazon and Ebay. As a result I was inveigled on to ITV against my better judgment to be interviewed by Janet Street-Porter and Auberon Waugh; a fogey lamb pushed to slaughter. Though a huge television addict as a small child, I have not watched the box much as a grown-up, never having had the time, being too busy, too social, too poly-domiciled, to be able to sit down and goggle for any length of time. I was a television innocent in the early 1980s. Nor have I made a point of appearing on television myself. It is a tedious and a flattening medium which excludes nuance and irony, and was extremely badly paid (unless one was a select star). In those days print journalism was more lucrative than hackwork for television. Making a programme in the 1970s with Arthur 'Bogus', the homely Cheltenham antique dealer who filled a popular slot talking about old furniture and 'stately' homes, put me off for life. The Negus-Robinson programme was about a house called Dodington in Gloucestershire and he was pretending to interview me as an architectural expert on the finer points: 'Is that a Corinthian column, John?' and 'What do you call that ledgy thing over there, John?'

It took all day, and we seemed to hang around for hours before any serious work began with armies of bored youngish people standing around chain-drinking coffee, while he tried to master such essentials as the name of the place. 'What's this house called, John?' 'Dodington'. Finally the cameras rolled and he began. 'Here we are today at Bodington.' CUT! He did it three times. I wanted to scream. The boredom. When I finally crawled back to London on a British Rail train in the evening gloom, I couldn't even console myself 'think of the money'. The fee for a whole day was a third of what even *Country Life* paid for an article at that time *and* at least their editor usually got the name of the house right.

Nevertheless, I agreed to do the interview with London Weekend Television in 1984, appearing on the 'Janet Street-Porter Show', to keep Alex happy. It was an embarrassing shock, but as the programme came out at the weekend I could console myself with the thought that nobody one knew would see it as they would all be in the country and too busy in the garden, or treating their dogs for ticks. Having never seen the show (though Janet was faintly familiar as she was married to an architect and they were doing up a cottage in the Yorkshire Dales), I did not know that she specialised in interviewing freaks, do-it-yourself witch doctors from Neasden and that type of thing. On my show the attention was shared with a humourless, American 'comedian' popping out of his too tight lumberjack shirt, an East End bricklayer with a taste for frightful frocks, and a fledgling 'pop star' who was proud of his lyrics like 'Sock it to me biscuit'. Never heard of again, it is probable that the world shared my low opinion of his talents.

In the Stamps drawing room in St Chad Street. Jonathan Glancey, Jonathan Meades and JMR, 1983. Note the unpainted plaster as background to framed architectural pictures (Gavin Stamp).

It was good cheerful stuff and I tried not to be too mesmerized by the Street-Porter teeth and phoney Cockney vowels, putting on a show of fogeyish courtesy worthy of Jacob Rees-Mogg and suppressing my natural irascibility. Afterwards at the 'social' Auberon Waugh told me I had 'done well'. He sympathised with my likely embarrassment, for he was as gentle in person as he was fierce in print. I had a good technical conversation with the stocky bricklayer-in-drag who was very proud of the number of courses he could lay in an hour, and waxed poetic about slopping mortar speedily back and forth on his trowel like a circus animal balancing a ball on its nose.

In the 1980s many of us were drawn towards the *Spectator* in Doughty Street and we attended the summer party there annually for over twenty years, and contributed from time to time, both general pieces and book reviews. Under the editorship of Alexander Chancellor it had become the best weekly magazine and everyone read it, whereas a generation earlier the *New Statesman* was better; the change was marked when Auberon Waugh and Paul Johnson were enticed to the former from the latter. The fact that a group of us had moved to live in Bloomsbury was also a factor. My house in Doughty Mews was acquired in 1982, the same year that Gavin and Alex Stamp moved to St Chad Street, off Argyle Square, opposite King's Cross Station. Another friend, Alan Powers, who had been a pupil of David Watkin at Cambridge and was an expert in 20th century architecture, with his wife Susanna, had bought a terraced late-Georgian house in Judd Street, north of Brunswick Square. They converted the shop on the ground floor into an art gallery where there were several exhibitions of works by artists in the Ravilious tradition. Alan himself, as well as being an architectural historian, was a talented artist and designer more in the Arts & Crafts tradition than the neo-Georgian. The Art Workers' Guild, founded by William Morris, was in Queen's Square, Bloomsbury, in an early-Georgian house and attracted Young as well as Old Fogeys.

Alan was introduced in 1979 through Glyn Boyd Harte, when they were both in the North of England and we visited a folly he had built and designed as a student in the holidays for friends. Glyn had started exhibiting his work successfully at Francis Kyle's Gallery in Cork Street in 1979, though they later fell out after Glyn tactlessly said that Kyle knew nothing about art and he would be better suited to flogging bibles in the Mid-West. Glyn was genuinely surprised that Francis took offence and refused to act for Glyn and his wife any further. Glyn and Carrie by that stage had also moved down-hill from Cloudesley Square in Islington to a vast mid-18th century house in Percy Street, off Charlotte Street, in what he called Fitzrovia, just the other side of Tottenham Court Road. They had finally finished Cloudesley Square by putting in a working kitchen in the basement. It was always the joke, that Glyn lost interest in restoring a house and sold it, the moment there was a kitchen. Not much chance of that for a long time in Percy Street where, while Glyn installed marble chimney-pieces in the manner of William Chambers and designed a grained Gothick library, the back wall fell out.

Glyn's exhibition at the Kyle Gallery was a flagrant flaunting of fantasies, a cosy apotheosis of personal tastes celebrating all his favourite themes in topography and still-life: Venice, Proust, Paris, glazed chintz, marble obelisks, tea pots, graining, grocer's green paint, red and white check table cloths, and Holland blind twilight. It contained his best work before declining health, lack of concentration, the depredations of the Inland Revenue, and the loss of a gallery to promote his art, took their toll. Glyn's pictures were to be found in all true 'fogey' abodes, and we all still have several of them hanging on the walls. He also re-designed and helped decorate our houses and generally contributed to a particular aesthetic with echoes of Janet Stone and John Piper which still flourishes and in its contemporary guise is captured in Ruth Guilding's 'Bible of British Taste' web site or Ben Pentreath's Bloomsbury shop. Glyn's work is recorded in his Royal College of Art contemporary Ian 'Archie' Beck's illustrated biography of him. Glyn had a gift for caricature, rapidly sketching friends at dinner, but did not develop that talent into regular cartoons which he would have been good at, though he did contribute the odd one to the *Spectator*.

Alan Powers designed a series of pen and ink colophon emblems or headings for the different sections in the *Spectator* which lasted for many years. Andrew Wilson became the Literary Editor. Charles Moore succeeded Alexander Chancellor as editor at the age of 28 in 1984, and James Knox, biographer of Robert Byron and Osbert Lancaster, (both fogey heroes) became the publisher of the magazine to complete the dominance of fogeydom. Of course, the then owner of the magazine, Algy Cluff, was an arch-fogey himself. Another ornament of the halcyon phase was Jennifer Paterson, who was taken on to cook the *Spectator's* Thursday lunches. She was later better known as one of the Two Fat Ladies on a motor bike with the alcoholic Clarissa Dickson Wright, in a television cookery programme put together for the BBC as an

"The Soanies" from the New Georgian Handbook, written on the floor at St Chad Street. Caricature illustration by Lawrence Mynott. Spot the Ravilious alphabet mug.

artificial construct like the Spice Girls (they disliked each other) by Patricia Llewellyn. (By a strange coincidence Patricia and her husband bought 14 Fournier Street after Eric Elstob's death, and completed its restoration.)

It is not clear that Jennifer could cook. Certainly when she came to stay she never did, and no-one was ever invited home to eat at the flat near Westminster Cathedral which she shared with her uncle Anthony Bartlett, *Gentiluomo* to the Cardinal Archbishop. At the *Spectator* her cooking career came to an abrupt end when

Jennifer Patterson while staying at Barbon, with JMR after Mass at Kirkby Lonsdale.

she threw all the coffee cups out of the window of the second floor kitchen into the neighbouring garden in Doughty Street and Charles Moore thought he ought to sack her as a danger to the lives of the local population. In an inspired move, he offered her a compensatory column writing 'Receipts' and that was the making of her, leading to cookery books, television and fame. A heavy drinker of vodka and whisky and non-stop cigarette smoker, she did not make it much beyond three score years and ten but died cheerfully, secure in her Catholicism. When someone went to see her in hospital and asked, rather idiotically, how she was, she responded loudly, 'Still dying'. At her Latin funeral in the Oratory her jewelled motor bike helmet was placed on her coffin.

Jennifer distributed bequests to many of her friends including to Clare Asquith at the *Spectator* who received the emerald ring (given Jennifer by Milo Keynes) which so mesmerized television viewers when she was mixing dough. I received a Victorian silver Stilton scoop, still known as the 'Jennifer Memorial Spoon'. Jennifer was an honorary Young Fogey though neither young nor a fogey. She was a natural actress with a strong assertive personality as a result of being the only girl in a family of boys to Army parents. Most of her acting went into her social life, but she also appeared occasionally in films. Her most uncharacteristic role, because silent and still, was in Derek Jarman's *Caravaggio* in 1986 where she appears under a sheet as one of the statues in Cardinal Del Monte's dust-sheeted Sculpture Gallery, an ingenious stroke of Christopher Hobbs' economical set design.

The Golden Age at the *Spectator* did not last. Charles Moore left in 1990 and went on to become editor of the *Daily Telegraph* and was succeeded by gloomy Dominic Lawson, and then by the lazy, amoral, ambitious, self-centred Boris Johnson who seemed to spend most of his time bonking Petronella Wyatt on the seat of a car in the garage in Brownlow Mews at the back. He left the other staff to write and produce the magazine while he promoted himself. To be fair though, he did take responsibility. When an entirely accurate editorial caused offence to Liverpool by describing its inhabitants as sentimental whingers wallowing in victimhood, there was uproar; he did a Canossa and went North to apologise in person, even though the piece had been written not by him but by Simon Heffer, another of the Fogeys. The *Spectator's* charm and brilliance departed and we more-or-less ceased to contribute. The *New Statesman* once again is the better magazine.

My connection with *Country Life*, however, has persisted for over 45 years through a series of American corporate owners, during which time I have written numerous articles on country houses, heraldry, book reviews and more general pieces. The first two articles, on the Wyatt family, were published in December 1973 as part of an application to be the staff architectural writer. John Cornforth, then the architectural editor, had approached David Watkin at Cambridge and Howard Colvin at Oxford to see if they could recommend a suitable young architectural historian. Howard recommended me, so one was summoned by Cornforth to the *Country Life* office in Covent Garden. It was still in the Lutyens building designed for the founder Edward Hudson. I ascended in a creaking old lift to the room of the architectural editor, still furnished with tables, chairs and a clock designed by Lutyens, and lined with books. My interviewer was a genial, snobbish, middle-aged Billy Bunter in a tweed suit, and all went well. I was offered the job. Meanwhile one had also been interviewed for a post in the ever to be lamented GLC Historic Buildings Division and offered that.

Job hunting is like waiting for a bus. Nothing happens for ages, then they all come along at once. Advice being sought of Howard Colvin, he said, 'you never know about magazines, they can be taken over and closed down, whereas with a public organisation you are assured of a long-term future.' In the event it was the GLC which was closed down. *Country Life*, although it has been taken over repeatedly by short-term multi-national owners and moved from one hideous open-plan concrete and glass office to another, is still going and making a multi-million dollar profit (not shared with the contributors). One architectural editor said, 'the ownership of this company is enough to make everyone a Communist'.

It was the right decision and instead of joining the *Country Life* desk staff, I became a retained architectural writer alongside Gervase Jackson-Stops and Richard Haslam. That is still the case, though no longer paid a monthly retainer because a transient American owner thought a retainer was an 'anachronism'. I didn't find it an anachronism; I liked being paid. The fee for the articles has not only not increased over the intervening near half-century, but has actually decreased in real terms. We keep at it though because *Country Life's* architectural articles are a small contribution to keeping alive the flame of English civilisation.

While not a journalist by profession, I have contributed innumerable pieces (usually written on the train between houses and jobs) to a range of papers and magazines over the years, including *Connoisseur* (defunct), the *Illustrated London News* (defunct), *Apollo* (not what it was), *History Today* (ditto), the *T.L.S.* (ditto), *Daily Telegraph*, etcetera. *Connoisseur* came through Bevis Hillier when he was editor. He used to take contributors to lunch in the Charing Cross or Great Western hotels on the grounds that his hero Betjeman (whose biography he eventually wrote) liked railway hotels. He was an expert on Art Deco when I met him at the Geffrye Museum in the 1970s. At *Apollo* there was a succession of sympathetic editors, Robin Simon, Anna Somers Cocks and Michael Hall. After she left, Anna founded the *Art Newspaper* with her Italian publisher husband Umberto Allemandi, and you can read there all the fascinating stories on museum mismanagement, illegal exports, art frauds, over-restoration scandals and the like, that do not reach the pages of the daily press. Michael Hall moved on to the *Burlington,* for which I have never written and regard it as a vehicle for interminable Germanic articles, suffering from foot and note disease, on the *pentimenti* in the left hand wing of a Florentine quattrocento triptych by an Unknown Master. It is admirable though, and one does admire seriousness in others.

History Today was briefly an organ of choice when a fellow Orielensis Michael Trend was editor, though he left when he became Conservative MP for Eton and Windsor. Two college friends became MPs. The other was Andrew Rowbotham, now a Cameron Life Peer. Andrew was MP for Blaby in Leicestershire after serving in the army, and so has always concerned himself in defence and security matters. Other Oriel politicians, Alan Duncan and Daniel Hannan, one a Remainer, the other a Leaver, were younger, but like all of us were encouraged in radical Tory ways by the Oriel history don and Senior Dean Jeremy Catto, a brilliant medieval historian. They were exceptions, as in general NOBODY of talent, ability or taste has gone into public politics for thirty years.

I was hugely touched later in reading a review by Jeremy: 'Orielenses of the 1970 generation will vividly remember the author of this book: a highly articulate redhead, defiantly civilized among the sartorial rebels of the age, deceptively mild in demeanour but in reality a seasoned fighter for the causes he cherishes ... In retrospect we can see that the early 1970s were the beginning of a more rational era of conservation, an epoch of hope to which John has made a decisive contribution.' I would have been happy to read that coming from anybody, but from Jeremy it was praise indeed so, immodestly, I share it with you.

Contributions to the *Daily Telegraph* came through Hugh Montgomery-Massingberd (dubbed Massive Snob by *Private Eye*), the brother of Mary Montgomery who was one of the members of the Oxford Gregorian Chant Society. When we first met, Hugh was the editor of Burke's *Peerage* and had embarked on an ambitious project to publish a series of volumes on all the country seats of Britain and Ireland. The work began well and Mark Bence Jones, much more of a massive snob than Hugh himself, whose seat at Glenville was the epitome of Irish Descendancy decay and disorder, produced a comprehensive volume on the whole island of Ireland. The volumes on the West-Worcestershire, Herefordshire and Shropshire—and the East-Essex, Suffolk, Cambridgeshire and Norfolk—also appeared, the former by Peter (Baronets) Reid—not to be muddled with Peter (Opera) Reid, the latter by John Kenworthy-Browne, David Watkin and Michael Sayer, a Norfolk landowner-fogey and expert on European nobility. Nicholas Kingsley, the archivist, began work on Gloucestershire which eventually came out under his own imprint in three volumes.

Hugh asked me to take on my native north-west-Lancashire, Cheshire, Cumberland and Westmorland (and the Isle of Man). I started work in 1973. It fitted perfectly with sojourns in the North and gave a focus for rural perambulations. I thought it would be my first book, and then for a time I feared it might be my last. Burke's went bankrupt, not once but three times. By that date Hugh had left. *Burke's Seats* shuddered to a halt. My work was completed and type-set but was still with the printers at Over Wallop in Hampshire. They refused to release the page proofs until they were paid. The money was not forthcoming and the text stayed firmly in the hands of BAS Printers Limited. Successive owners of Burke's made no effort to relieve the log jam as they were too busy wasting money on logos and parties. Over a decade passed and then the copyright reverted to me and Hugh under the terms of the original contract. Through Nicholas Robinson (not a relation but a friend, and great-nephew of Jim Lees-Milne) who had recently joined Constable's, we approached Ben Glazebrook, Constable's chairman, and explained the predicament. It was pointed out that if Constables paid the printing bill they could have the text and would receive a book in print state ready for immediate publication at little cost to themselves. They did, and *Country Houses of the North West* came out belatedly in 1991. It was a business coup for them and sold out immediately with little financial outlay by Constable beyond settling an old printing bill diminished substantially over the years by inflation.

Working with Hugh was fun despite the uncertain outcome, and vicissitudes along the way. His humour made the job enjoyable, and as part of his editing Hugh inserted amusing stories and gossip about some of the former owners, ensuring that the text was not dry-as-dust history. (I refer the reader to the financially incontinent Earl of Lathom who was requested by the Ritz to pay the bill for his wedding reception in advance.) Hugh's policy was to include a photograph of every house, however dim the image, for as he said, 'one picture is worth a hundred words'. The uneven quality of the illustrations was overcome by the design of Humphrey Stone who kept the ancient grey snaps as small as postage stamps while giving prominent half pages to the good photographs, especially those of *Country Life* or others taken for the book by young photographers such as the late Angus Taylor (biographer of the Westmorland architect George Webster) and Cressida Pemberton-Piggot (now Lady Inglewood). The prominent use of *Country Life* photographs caused a further problem as the magazine had changed hands and the original arrangement to provide the photos to Burke's had been forgotten. The then transient owners demanded a large reproduction fee, which we couldn't afford, but as the author was a regular contributor of theirs, they eventually waived this and kept to the original agreement, though not without first taking legal advice which warned them they might *not* have a strong case.

The layout and design meetings took place in Humphrey's barn studio adjoining his handsome Victorian farmhouse at Lower

Lawn, Fonthill in Wiltshire, an appropriate architectural setting, and very enjoyable. I would go down for the day to Tisbury by train to that magical landscape of West Wiltshire and North Dorset with all its architectural treasures, an area comparable to the Veneto in terms of houses, but with countryside less spoilt by unplanned modern development, rubbish tipping, light pollution, and concrete mess.

Editorial meetings with Hugh were also fun as they took place over lunch at the Travellers, for which Hugh had been put up by his cousin Peter Montgomery of Blessingbourne in County Tyrone, Northern Ireland. Peter Montgomery was President of the Northern Ireland Arts Council. For a time Hugh was considered the heir (Peter had paid his school fees at Harrow), but in the event the estate was left to another nephew. Hugh's parents answering for him, turned it down, as they also did the family's right to live at Gunby in Lincolnshire which had been given to the National Trust by Field Marshal Massingberd and which Hugh loved. So Hugh was a bit of a displaced squire in London, but every summer he and his wife 'Ripples' house-sat at Gunby when the National Trust tenant was on holiday and it was wonderful to be with them there and see Hugh in his ancestral setting in the panelled rooms and the beautiful Edwardian gardens. It was like the opening shots of 'The Go Between'. Hugh was a great trencherman and at Gunby much time and thought went into dinner, as we sat on the steps facing the garden, drinking in the evening sun.

At the Travellers Hugh was the hero of the kitchen as he always had double helpings of bread sauce with his partridge and both pudding *and* savoury at lunch and dinner. His love of heavy food was his downfall and he had a heart attack after cooking and eating a massive Christmas dinner of pork and crackling and potatoes roasted in goose fat.

Alas, he barely made it to sixty, but saw his eldest grandson born. He very kindly proposed me for the Travellers. I was seconded by Edward Lidderdale, son of the Clerk to the Commons, and duly elected in 1978, so have been a member now for over forty years. I always think of Hugh when dining there in Barry's splendid Coffee Room, often at the 'Monsignor's table' where Alfred Gilbey sat into his nineties. The current ghosts at the club are quite recent and have largely superseded the eminent Victorians.

After Hugh left Burke's he joined the *Telegraph* as obituaries editor. This was the perfect job for him with his passion for genealogy and families, and delight in human foibles. Previously second fiddle to the *Times*, the *Telegraph* obits were vastly improved by him. Hugh's horse overtook on the inside track and was soon racing ahead (he had a fondness for the gee-gees, and tended to place his book advances on the Turf). He invented the modern newspaper obituary with a frankness, wit and liveliness hitherto lacking. More to the point, he built up a stable of regular contributors with different specialisms: a couple of retired soldiers and RAF men to do 'the moustaches', heroes of the Second World War reaching the end of their natural term; or bohemians with contemporary knowledge to cover 'popular musicians M'Lud', who tended to pop off young—drugs, drink, sex and car crashes; and Hugh asked me to write up one or two figures from the worlds of architecture and heraldry.

Hugh wanted pieces to put on ice for the future as well as more urgent pieces on people who had died that morning. I found the obituary format very difficult when writing in cold blood for stock. It was much easier dashing something off for the evening deadline. Even so, I may still have one or two Hugh-commissioned pieces on file, like delayed depth charges. One did one's best to be tactful as well as truthful but even so it was possible to cause offence. My obituary of Colin Cole, Garter King of Arms, hard drinking and not über-efficient, an officer of a distinguished Foot Regiment in the War, and later a Territorial Colonel, ruffled some feathers. We quoted The Queen's Private Secretary's note attached to a Garter Patent to the effect that 'Her Majesty preferred to sign such documents while the recipient was still alive', referring to a Knight who had expired during the endless ages that the necessary paperwork had taken to emerge from Cole's office. It shone a not unfavourable light on all concerned, but a successor (efficient) Garter was not amused. Nevertheless, we enjoyed some vindication when *my* obituary (not one of the blander rivals) was reprinted almost verbatim in the *Guards Magazine*.

One of the high points of Hugh's obit editorship was his outings to suitable places—a country graveyard in Shropshire, or an historic church with magnificent heraldry and angel bedecked family tombs, and lunch. The one I remember best was a trip to Northern France to see the Commonwealth War Graves. We crossed the Channel and first had a slap-up lunch in the best restaurant in Boulogne. Course followed elaborate course and bottle after bottle. We never got to the military cemeteries. Hugh suddenly looked at his watch and said, 'Oh dear, the home ferry is due, there is just time for a last glass of brandy. We must come back another day.' We never did.

Travellers lunches were a bit like that too, if not so rumbustious because of the presence of Monsignor Alfred Gilbey, dressed either in a clerical frock coat or the violet cinctured cassock of a Prelate, a Monsignor Proto Notary Apostolic, for he was a member of the Papal Court. Such an echo of Rome seemed wholly appropriate in the setting of Barry's Italianate architecture. In a way, the Monsignor was much more the Honorary Patron saint of the Young Fogeys than the Prince of Wales. As Catholic Chaplain at Cambridge for one hundred terms from 1933 to 1965, where he had successfully preserved Edwardian mores, he had retired to Club land in St James's, when his world was seemingly overthrown for a time by the Second Vatican Council. The Travellers changed its rules after he was elected in March 1965 so that he could live there continuously, and the club became his home for thirty-three years, almost until he died in 1998. A boot room in the attic was converted to his private chapel and survives to this day, a unique amenity in a London club.

Alfred was responsible for introducing many new members to the club, undergraduates he had known at Cambridge, or their sons and grandsons, and traditionalist dons, notably his special protégé and friend the late David Watkin who was Professor of Architectural History at Cambridge and a notable proponent of modern Classical architecture in the work of Craig Hamilton, Quinlan Terry, John Simpson and Robert Adam, and their younger disciples.

I first met David at a lecture he gave on C.R. Cockerell at the RIBA Drawings Collection in 1971 where the wittily delivered architectural information was enlivened by social background and personal details such the beauty of Cockerell's countenance as described in the Passport for his travel to Greece and the Levant signed by Castlereagh, and the wonderful portrait drawing by Ingres. Alfred sat at the back reading his breviary throughout as if oblivious to the verbal fireworks. It was a staggering contrast to my old tutor Howard Colvin whose careful and meticulous scholarship had never made me want to smile, though I admired it and have tried to live up to his standards in my historical research.

When visiting Cambridge, David's rooms in St Peter's Terrace were a regular draw. They were a *piano nobile* set with library, dining room, boot room and bedroom, full of books, Jacobite portraits, a grand piano, Regency furniture and neo-Classical objects in the style of Thomas Hope, his aesthete hero and subject of his PhD Thesis and first book. The late Roger Scruton in the eulogy at David's funeral in King's Lynn in 2018 remembered them as 'the chambers of a Regency gentleman with furnishings, prints and ornaments that might have been rescued from a great estate ... It had the air of someone who had fallen from the heights of inherited affluence and was struggling to maintain himself in elegant decline.' That was not for me their most memorable feature.

There were often bright amusing guests, and discussions were irreverent, reactionary, radical, and witty. I remember calling mid-morning on a Saturday in term-time and there were a couple of hung-over people who had stayed on the floor after a club dinner the night before (possibly the Strafford dining club in homage to Charles I's brilliant, martyred statesman). One was Rory O'Donnell, a pupil of David, who went on to work for English Heritage, and became an arch-fogey. The other was an American undergraduate who was in the bath. David introduced him through the open door as we passed and instead of just nodding and carrying on scrubbing, the boy stood up and gravely shook my hand, dripping like a seal, as if at a formal reception in 1910 rather than full frontal nude. Upper class Americans have much better manners than the English, more unaffected, with seemingly charming simplicity or is it knowing-ness? We all went out to the pub at Trumpington for lunch, and I never saw him again, with or without clothes.

David Watkin had been greatly influenced by Alfred and had adopted many sartorial mannerisms and Edwardian shibboleths from him, as well as converting to Catholicism. David in turn, together with a covey of Right Wing Peterhouse dons, and John Casey at Caius (founder of the Conservative Philosophy Group), reacted against the trendy nostrums of 1960s academe, adopting a contrary traditionalist stance on almost everything, that they passed on to their pupils. Alan Powers, Gavin Stamp, Rory O'Donnell, Clive Aslet (later editor of *Country Life* and journalist), Hugh Roberts (later Director of the Royal Collection), and the majority of the Fogey Host derived their distinctive counter-revolutionary leopards spots from that source. One could see before one's eyes a three-generation Apostolic Succession.

David was a very clever and determined anti-modernist and his book *Morality and Architecture* (1977) destroyed the Determinist philosophical underpinning of the Modern Movement as promoted by academics and architects, and its fallacious zeitgeist analogies with Science and Socialism. It was met with outrage by the architectural establishment entrenched in the RIBA (a trade union for mediocrities posing as an educational and cultural charity) and the Schools of Architecture. But it inspired a pop song with the same title and was an inspiration to the Prince of Wales and his encouragement of traditional architecture. Interestingly, with the passage of time, the thesis of David's polemic has become an established norm and nobody disagrees with it now, not even architectural students.

David was seen by some of his university colleagues as an 'evil reactionary, an enemy of social progress and enlightenment', to quote Scruton who was thrilled that a person like that should have been given a fellowship at all. Such good news seemed barely credible. David saw himself as 'part of a pocket of resistance to change, firmly anchored in classical architecture and the church', the foundations which Alfred Gilbey had helped him to construct when an undergraduate at Trinity Hall. Like Scruton, I too found all this most sympathetic, being temperamentally reactionary myself and rooted in my case, by heredity and upbringing, in the Catholic Church. I too had detached doubts about the Americanised twilight of the Enlightenment which tinctured the late-20th century. It may not survive the absolutist, patriarchal, religious and cultural influences of Islam or Chinese imperialism which can be expected to subvert and supersede the materialist, secularist and egalitarian culture of modern society in the West.

My own working life in the 1970s and early 1980s was spent in the Leftist GLC where we worked whole-heartedly on public spirited schemes like the grand conservation programme for Covent Garden and Seven Dials, converting the fruit and vegetable warehouses to mixed residential, and the old market buildings to small shops, restaurants, workshops and tourist boutiques. Much of our effort was also devoted to assisting Housing Associations and local authority conversions of Georgian terraces into social housing in Camden, Islington, Hackney, Tower Hamlets, Southwark, Bermondsey and Lambeth; guiding their architects and helping with funding. This secured the survival of whole swathes of historic inner London while providing attractive affordable flats and houses. When Ken Livingstone took over as Leader of the Council in the 1980s, we expected him to be anti-historic buildings and conservation. But in the event that was not the case. A wily politician, he realised that the Historic Buildings Division with its Blue Plaques and grants was one of the popular bits of the Council and so threw money at it to dish out and buy him, he hoped, political favour.

As a result we were able to give grants to the Travellers Club for restoring Barry's original scheme of oak graining in the library and to the Brompton Oratory church for reinstating a Victorian scheme of blue and gold stencilled decoration inside the dome, all very good socialist causes. I am always amused by the indiscriminate impact of grant schemes; just as later, EU-originated Higher Level Stewardship grants for agriculture, intended to assist French peasants in small holdings, were hugely diverted to English dukes to help restore and replant their Capability Brown parks spreading over thousands of acres.

Nemesis for the Historic Buildings Division came from another direction entirely, from the Right not the Left. Livingstone's attempts to buy political favour did not work. His admittedly childish posturings, attracted the wrath of Mrs Thatcher and she abolished the GLC, including our poor little Historic Buildings Division, with dire long-term results for London, opening the way for a trashed skyline and a tide of third rate commercial and tourist tat. From my own point of view it ended a career in public service and diverted my activities into other more personal areas of interest and alternative lives.

I was also idiotic enough to take my pension out of the Civil Service Pension scheme to which we were attached, and put it into a dud Hill Samuel private pension as advised by a dodgy broker. Influenced by early Thatcherite optimism, one might as well have thrown the money into the sea. It would have been more fun watching it bobbing on the waves than helplessly studying the downward graphs to financial ruin and disaster. Fortunately I am not entirely dependent in old age on a pension, but its loss was a salutary warning that it is always better *to do nothing*, and never to follow 'good advice'. Gentle inaction is the best policy for nearly all things, as wise old bird the 3rd Marquess of Salisbury, Queen Victoria's last and greatest Prime Minister, understood so well in the *fin de siècle*; pity his policies have not been followed in succeeding centuries.

3
Travels with Woodrow

MY FIRST PROPER book to be published was *The Wyatts*, a publication on the whole architectural dynasty of over two dozen architects as well as inventors and land agents, sculptors and painters, and other remarkable people. They spanned the one and a half centuries between the 1730s and 1880s which saw the apogee of British industrial, agricultural and maritime expansion. I say my first proper book, as my first publication, in 1978, was a limited edition of the *Observations on the Theory and Practice of Landscape Gardening* by Humphry Repton, a reprint of Repton's own publication complete with his famous aquatint flaps showing landscapes before and after 'Improvement'. This was produced

JMR at Doughty Mews, surrounded by the Wyatts. Benjamin Dean Wyatts' unexecuted plans for Waterloo Palace for the Duke of Wellington. (Getty Images).

for a small collectors' market of 445 copies printed in fourteen colours, with a handsome slip case and leather-spined binding; each volume cost £400 (nearly a quarter of my GLC salary). I still have my own copy and it is very handsome with its marbled endpapers and cream laid paper, but I do not know how many of the 445 copies were sold. It has sunk beneath the waves.

The Wyatts on the other hand was a proper commercial product, published by Oxford University Press, the first of four books I did for them in the 1980s. It still sells on ABE for four or five times the publication price. It grew out of my DPhil thesis on Samuel Wyatt. I approached the Press and asked them if they would be interested in publishing a book on Sam, as he was a talented neo-Classical architect and engineer whose career seemed to embody many of the themes of the British Enlightenment and the Industrial Revolution. They thought Sam would be too narrow for the general market and could the book be developed to cover the whole Wyatt dynasty which would give a wider picture of English Georgian and Victorian culture and achievement. It seemed a daunting prospect requiring a large amount of extra research, but I agreed. The prospect was complicated by the fact that my American friend and colleague Fran Fergusson who had written her PhD thesis on James Wyatt, Sam's protean younger brother, under Professor Ackerman at Harvard was intending to develop that into a monograph on James Wyatt, the most talented of the whole Wyatt family. We discussed it, and there seemed not too much cross-over as I would only include one chapter on James, with the majority of the book on all the other Wyatts. In some ways my project would be an introduction to hers. We worked happily together, and shared results. I stayed with her and her then husband, the medieval historian Peter Fergusson, a scholar of English medieval monasteries, at Wellesley, Massachusetts, as well as in London where they had a mews house in Notting Hill.

As it turned out, Fran in the course of her career became one of the American 'Great and the Good': President of Vassar College, where she raised $750 million in a successful fund-raising campaign, and employed Cesar Pelli to design new buildings, Governor of New York School of Ballet, a Trustee of the Ford Foundation, Chairman of the Mayo Clinic and a member of the board of the Getty Trust, and much else, so in the event she never had the time to publish her monograph on 'our James' as we called him. Forty years later and with extraordinary generosity, she sent me a large Fedex parcel with all her research notes and photographs. In 2013 I eventually published James Wyatt's architectural biography based on our joint work to coincide with the bicentenary of his death in a carriage accident on Salisbury Plain in 1813.

In 1973 I focussed on a history of 'Wyatts Galore' as Debo Devonshire referred to my researches in the archives at Chatsworth. With the Wyatts I benefited from a huge stroke of luck and generosity, for as I was agreeing with OUP to do the book I was approached by Woodrow Wyatt who wanted to commission a family history. He was descended from William Wyatt, Sam and James's elder brother and indeed from all the other Wyatts as nine of them married their first cousins in the 19th century in a characteristic cosy Victorian attempt to keep the genius and money in the family. Woodrow had approached Hugh Trevor-Roper for a recommendation of a young historian and he proposed me.

By coincidence, my Oxford friends included Robbie Lyle, Woodrow's nephew whose father had changed his name to Lyle on inheriting the Bonython estate in Cornwall, and who was also at Oriel, and Nicholas Banszky, Woodrow's Hungarian stepson by his fourth marriage to Verushka Banszky, so I found myself drawn into the ambit of the modern as well as the historic Wyatt family, and this turned out to be a very rewarding and jolly experience. Woodrow paid me an annual retainer and expenses, let me use his country house, Conock Old Manor in Wiltshire as a retreat when I was writing the book. He paid for all the illustrations, commissioning Patrick Lichfield and his charming brother-in-law Geoffrey Shakerley to take the photographs of Wyatt buildings specially. I am extremely grateful. Woodrow treated me as another eccentric nephew and I grew very fond of him in all his larger than life exuberance with his cigars, bow tie and vintage champagne. Though we sparred, it was friendly sparring and I was never the butt of his umbrageous side. He reserved that for journalist and political rivals; and he could be very rude to them, making enemies. By contrast I found him shrewd, funny and warm-hearted.

He was a controversial figure among his contemporaries, and his ruthlessly indiscreet *Journals* published in 1988, 1999 and 2000 (he died in 1997) damaged his posthumous reputation, but he wrote them with the excellent intention of providing a pension from their royalties and sales for his widow Verushka after his death, as he was unable to leave her much else, his business ventures having failed. Many old friends were upset and his enemies regarded him as a ghastly social-climber and political turn-coat, socialist-turned-Thatcherite. In one of the less unfriendly reviews, Geoffrey Levy wrote 'How terribly unfair on Woodrow (Lord) Wyatt to judge him by his conversations with the famous, jotted down night after night with questionable accuracy in his diary and now being published. The Queen Mother, Princess Michael of Kent, prime ministers, dukes ... How much fairer to remember the man for himself ... the pomposity, his towering self-aggrandisement and social climbing ...'

Woodrow certainly liked dukes. I am quite keen on them myself, especially their houses, so that seems a very venial sin. His political career was more consistent than was allowed by critics. After serving in the army in the Second World War and being promoted to Major, he did a stint in India as Personal Assistant to Stafford Cripps on the Cabinet Mission in 1946, while being elected for Parliament as Labour MP for Aston, then Bosworth in the Midlands from 1945 to 1970. He was Parliamentary Under-Secretary for War in 1951. His real parliamentary work, however, with Ted Knight was to expose the Marxist threat in the British Unions, especially the communist infiltration of the Electricians' Union. His belief in the necessity for union reform and private enterprise led to his support in due course for Margaret Thatcher, a completely consistent and understandable course. She became a confidante and gave him a peerage, though he sat in the Lords as a Cross Bencher, and began to have doubts about her as she succumbed to irrationality and madness in her later premiership years. He loved the trappings though. I had lunch with him soon after he became Lord Wyatt of Weeford, and he had spent all morning in Jermyn Street ordering a pair of crested and coroneted slippers to wear with his smoking jacket in the evening.

Woodrow also always believed firmly in the private manufacturing economy, reflecting the Wyatt roots in the industrial Midlands. Arnold Weinstock at GEC was his hero. Woodrow, with his fellow Labour MP Desmond Donnelly, had saved the steel industry from being re-nationalised in Harold Wilson's Labour Government in the 1960s when he and Donnelly withheld their vital votes and the Nationalisation Bill was narrowly defeated in the Commons. His principal achievement was the printing business W.W. Web Offset that he developed in Banbury with brother Major Robert Lyle, a financier with de Zoete & Bevan (the stockbroking house that Eric Elstob also worked in). Woodrow Wyatt bought the local newspaper, the *Banbury Guardian*; and introduced off-set litho printing there. This was a cheaper, faster printing technique to replace hot metal, which Woodrow had witnessed on a parliamentary visit to the USA and brought back to England.

We sometimes visited the Works in Banbury and the process was impressive with its gleaming modern machinery, computers and hundreds of staff. For a time it was a success, and Web Offset printed all the English telephone directories, among other things, but the business was dented when Woodrow divorced his third wife Lady Moorea Hastings (daughter of the left wing artist-earl, Jack Huntingdon) and she took her capital out with her, leaving him with bank debt. The business never recovered and eventually failed, but Woodrow continued to live like the millionaire he had for a time become, with his rosy brick early-Georgian house near Devizes and an ample stucco Italianate villa in St John's Wood, a large gold-coloured, chauffeur-driven Mercedes and succession of Italian/Hungarian butlers.

After the Web Offset debacle, he kept afloat in his later years as perpetual chairman of the Tote Board, the nationalised arm of racecourse betting, which he chaired for 21 years, with a salary, car, and lavish entertaining expenses. He did not know a vast amount about racing, I suspect, but he had shares in horses, and a penchant for the grander, richer owners: the Devonshires, Derbys, Marlboroughs, Beauforts and Weinstocks. We sometimes went with him to Newbury where Jeremy Tree, son of Nancy Lancaster of Colefax & Fowler fame was the steward. I shared Woodrow's interest in the hospitality tent and atmosphere, less in the field, finding modern flat-racing a bit of a bore. I prefer jumps as in the Holcombe Harriers point-to-point or Cartmel Races in Lancashire of my childhood, much more eighteenth-century experiences. At the former we knew the man who did the 'score board' and who let us climb up as children to watch from his elevated platform; not just the races as it turned out, but also the shooting of horses that fell at jumps and broke their legs, because we could see down over the canvas screens erected to hide the shocking scenes on the ground.

Woodrow formally commissioned me to write the Wyatt family history in 1974. The arts editor of OUP, Jon Stalworthy, (an expert on Wilfred Owen and the First World War poets), with whom I had opened discussions had moved on by then, and John Bell became my loyal editor at the Press. As he said wryly, it was a case of youth giving way to age as he was Stalworthy's senior by a number of years. He was friendly and encouraging, and a novice writer could not have had a more amiable and supportive editor. Both of us went to a preliminary lunch at Woodrow's Italianate palazzo near Lords Cricket Ground in May 1974. The interior was striking with rich deep colours, thick rugs, lots of gilding and shiny white marble statues of the Venus de Milo and friends, embowered in Constance Spry flower arrangements, and a large piano. There were gold framed pictures, but none that I would have regarded as 'art'.

It was a bit of a joke when there was a burglary at Conock

once, after they had left for London on Sunday evening leaving the door wide open. The burglars had only taken the television set and ignored a painting labelled 'Gainsborough' hanging on the wall above it. I thought to myself 'what discerning burglars'. If the marble paved entrance hall and gilded drawing room in London set the Curzon Street Baroque tone, it reached a climax in the dining room. There was no timid pastel-tinted good taste at Cavendish Avenue where the colours were nearly as strong as the pervasive cigar smoke. I noted at the time, 'Woodrow's dining room is rather peculiar. It has ankle deep gold carpets and purple walls, with a service lift popping up through the floor and an Italian butler stacking in the basement kitchen then rushing upstairs to unload as the gold WW monogrammed plates arrive in the room with a loud crash.' Once there was an accident, and the whole load swooshed back down to the basement and smashed into smithereens.

We had 1946 champagne before lunch out of silver goblets, an excellent claret, and an ancient port after. All three of us were soon very drunk and grandiose idea followed grandiose idea. 'Why not ask Patrick Lichfield to take the photographs? He lives in a Wyatt house and Wyatts were land agents at Shugborough for three generations.' Woodrow's grandfather, great-grandfather and great-great-grandfather had been almost hereditary agents to the Lichfields in Staffordshire for nearly the whole of the 19th century. Woodrow talked of his business in Banbury. 'I know nothing about printing, I merely employ 650 printers ... we have works in London, Daventry, Banbury and Middlesborough ... I have no money. If only John Wyatt (the C18 inventor) had been more business-like we would have been rich ...' It set the tone for many future lunches held there including one with Patrick Lichfield, in a monogrammed and coroneted shirt, and who did indeed agree to do the photographs.

I was soon making regular visits all over the country, some in Woodrow's company which was often hilarious if he was in a good mood, some on my own via his introductions. In September 1974, on Woodrow's recommendation, I went to see Colonel Claud Lancaster at Kelmarsh Hall in Northamptonshire. He had recently built a new pair of entrance lodges to a long-lost design by James Wyatt. I found the idea of a brand new Wyatt building especially intriguing. The Colonel collected me from Kettering station and drove me to Kelmarsh, making conversation and cracking Edwardian jokes all the way. 'Oh, in my time at Oxford the only things that were safe at Keble were hedgehogs.' As a JP he pretended to be concerned about the rapid spread of incest from Rothwell (pronounced Row-well) to Kettering. His other obsession was the political and military weakness of the Americans: 'Sooner or later, we'll have to take the United States over again.' He did not drink but provided me with my own half bottle of excellent claret at lunch—true hospitality. The food was inedible—an over-done steak like a lump of cast iron. The lodges were and are perfect. Nobody would guess that they were built *circa* 1970 rather than *circa* 1770.

Through Woodrow, I first visited Badminton in October 1974, in pursuit of Wyatville—a very Lees-Milne experience. Caroline Somerset took us from The Cottage where she and David lived, over to the Big House which had a marvellous atmosphere of faded grandeur—long corridors upstairs full of wonky chests and rare Chinese porcelain. Mary Duchess who showed us around was wearing gumboots inside the house. She was elderly and sweet. We met her in the garden picking grass and walking seven dogs. As a 'flock' of ducks came towards us she shooed them away: 'Not now sillies, I'll feed you later.' Her sitting room was full of dogs' baskets and a parrot in a cage, with messes of boiled eggs in Meissen saucers on marble topped side tables to feed the animals. The room had elaborate oak panelling and carvings rescued from Raglan Castle (destroyed in the Civil War). Her conversation was laced still with admirable anti-Cromwell sentiment.

The great staircase had been enlarged and rearranged by Wyatville. She showed me the finely moulded tread ends and made me feel them, 'I'd never noticed them till I fell over going up one day and my nose came into contact with the carving.' There was a general atmosphere of feudal insouciance—disorder and lavishness—with huge vases of flowers, vast banks and pyramids of them everywhere. In the large dining room with its Grinling Gibbons carvings, one place was laid at the table. Her Grace's Secretary was summoned: 'Bywater, will you show the Professor to the Muniment Room.' I was merely an ex-graduate student, but it is always a good social technique to over-promote. Queen Mary had arranged the muniment room situated in a William Kent pavilion during her evacuation from London to Badminton in the War and the bundles were all tied neatly with pink ribbon and had cards of the contents written in the royal hand: 'Wyatville's building bills, 1806. Mary R.I.' They left me to my own devices and I walked back to The Cottage for lunch with the Somersets afterward. It was historical research *de luxe*. Woodrow was good friends with David and Caroline and remained so after they succeeded and moved to the Big House. His diaries lay in the future (he only started keeping them in the 1980s) and the sky was cloudless in the 1970s, the food delicious, the charm irresistible.

Woodrow often invited me for the weekend to his house near Devizes. Sometimes I caught the train to Wiltshire, but occasionally I went to Banbury and got a lift with him in the Mercedes, as he often spent Fridays at the Works. I would sit in the front with the driver, exercising my despised topographical skills while Woodrow sat in the back smoking a cigar with the newspapers and business files scattered on the seat beside him. The country house had charm. Woodrow did not own the freehold but leased it from a rich almshouse charity in Newbury. Conock looked like a doll's house, red brick with a hipped roof. The Georgian façade is dated 1751 in the brickwork headers. There was a field in front—called 'the park'—full of Jacob's sheep, one of which we ate for dinner on my first visit there. The interior was as outré as Cavendish Avenue, white wall-to-wall, with Aubusson rugs to catch your feet in, fluted 'marble' columns upholding gold-painted lamps, life-size plaster statues from the Great Exhibition, and all the brass doorknobs were his own portrait complete with glasses. Woodrow's library upstairs had an especially strong smell of cigars and tall bookcases with 20th century first editions, of which he was very proud. He had a tantrum, I remember, when he discovered that the cleaner had pushed the books back into the shelves—he liked them lined up at the front, so the air could circulate behind and neater-looking. He used to lean out of the window and shout to the gardener: 'Gunthorpe! Gunthorpe! The grass needs cutting.' Gunthorpe below was not fazed, and continued shambling around with lackadaisical gait.

There were several jaunts to Weeford in Staffordshire, the Wyatt place of origin, their 'stem seat' except that it was an old farmhouse not a seat. Visits included occasions like the village fête which Woodrow opened with panache, or the graveyard to choose his grave close to the ancestors. Petronella, with a little girl's logic said: 'Why do you want to be buried so far away?' 'Because the view of the fields is so pretty.' 'But you won't be able to see them.' Often Robbie and Nicholas would come on these adventures. On one hilarious occasion the Mercedes broke down at a roundabout, and the denizens of Staffordshire were treated to the sight of a large gold-coloured car with a small bow-tied man in the back puffing a cigar while the three of us and the driver pushed the defective vehicle to safety at the side of the road.

One such jaunt was in August 1975. It was a hectic visit. We drove up the motorway in the Mercedes at over 100 mph all the way and did a dash round Lichfield Cathedral, Shugborough, Weeford Church and Swinfen Hall (then a prison). Shugborough has an attractive interior—neo-Classical rooms by Sam Wyatt of varied shapes and size, all beautifully decorated and furnished. Only one buttress of James Wyatt's survived the Victorians at Lichfield. It was a pity that Swinfen was surrounded by a high barbed wire fence like something in a zoo. Then we dashed quickly back down the Fosse Way to Wiltshire through a landscape of dead and dying elm trees.

On Sunday we went to Fonthill Abbey, where the site of the James Wyatt house and a large model of Beckford's building, belonged to Neil Rimington. We got lost and I stopped to ask a keeper if it was the right way to Neil Rimington's. Woodrow was

Fonthill Abbey

shocked by this and said I should have referred to 'Mr Rimington'. He was always wonderfully generous and beneath the gruff cigar-waving exterior lay a kind-hearted soul. On that occasion he gave Robbie, Nicholas and me a bottle of champagne to take back to London with us, which we drank on our return with boiled eggs in Robbie's house in Princes Gate Mews, near the V&A.

In the years I visited Conock regularly between 1974 and 1978, the house remained much the same as Woodrow had created it when Moorea was his wife. Verushka did not change anything. It was very much Woodrow's country house. She did not like it, nor the wet muddy landscape of the north Wiltshire plain and vales. Verushka preferred Italy and her own house at Pisa. The lease of Conock was surrendered, after Woodrow came round to her point of view, and they moved to a summer retreat near Siena, selling the Pisa house, renting and doing up *La Cerbaia* at Cetinale in Tuscany. Woodrow took it from Tony Lambton on a seemingly good deal where, instead of the rent, he restored and maintained the buildings and paid the staff, but it all ended badly with a spectacular row over the swimming pool. The Wyatts left Cerbaia in a cloud of reciprocal vituperation in 1986, with Woodrow fuming: 'The trouble with Tony is he has an enthusiasm for people for a bit and then he turns against them,' and 'I think I shall make him the centre of a play if I write another one.'

By 1976, Conock was beginning to be a bit frayed. One of the dangers of staying there was the possibility of breaking your neck by catching your foot in the costly tatters of the Aubusson rugs strewn across the floors. The deference shown to a scruffy student-type was disconcerting. I was exactly the same as usual—the same jeans and same moth-eaten pullover, speaking in the same way. Yet when there I was treated to 'Yes sir, No Sir, Very good Sir' by everyone from the postman to the cook, not what one was used to in the decaying streets of 1970s socialist London. At lunch one day Mrs Macmillan said to me of Mrs Codrington of Dodington (a James Wyatt house I had recently visited), 'She has masses of taste—none of it good.' Woodrow fled to Birch Grove in Sussex with them on Saturday to stay with Harold Macmillan, leaving me to get on with my writing and fend for myself.

There was a storm which blew down three or four beech trees in the park and cut off all the electricity. We were left without light, heat or food and I had to cope on my own with the dipso', poofy cook (who claimed he was suffering from shell-shock and certainly behaved as if he was) and Verushka's aged, Hungarian mother who lived there in a cottage and understandably, stayed in bed all day. Woodrow had warned me that the cook was a 'bit eccentric'. Nevertheless I was slightly surprised when at 2pm no lunch had been announced. When I went down to find out what was happening he was crouching over the drawing room fire trying to keep warm, moaning to himself. When I said I would like something to eat, he replied that he couldn't cook anything as there was no electricity, but he managed to supply a few biscuits and some Brie (my least favourite cheese). In fact there was a large pot of Irish stew in the kitchen which could easily have been warmed up on the oil stove, and when I opened the fridge it was crammed with cold lamb, melon, apple pie etc. none of which he had seen fit to offer us. The last half hour before Woodrow left, we spent locking up the gin and wine so that the cook could not get at it. He drank anything left out in the house. I noticed that there were always some open bottles of beer on the kitchen table when he was cooking. He eloped just before Christmas with a waiter from a Heathrow hotel. It was not a success and he had returned to Conock begging to be taken on again.

I spent New Year 1976 and again Easter that year at Conock, which were among the most memorable stays there, partly because Roy and Jennifer Jenkins visited at New Year. Roy was an old colleague of Woodrow's from the Wilson Labour Party and Home Secretary; he had just appointed Woodrow chairman of the Tote Board. The Home Secretary was wearing an old tweed coat patched at the elbows with leather and looking like a country gent. I was slightly surprised. He was not as urbane or witty as I expected but pompously uncomfortable in company. He spent much of the time pontificating *very seriously* about the wine, which he managed to get wrong. [In his diary, Woodrow tells us that it was 1940 Chateau Latour.] Mrs Jenkins, by contrast, was fun. I liked her. She was chairman of the Historic Buildings Council and later the National Trust. We ate quails eggs with melon and shrimps, roast pheasant, baked applies. To drink: vintage champagne, good hock with the shrimps, 1940 Latour with the pheasant and then port. Lunch went on till 4 o'clock. I enjoyed it.

While at Conock that time I scored a black. Woodrow was showing me the typescript of a children's book he had just written for his daughter Petronella called *The Exploits of Mr Saucy Squirrel*. I said, 'Oh how interesting. Is it an autobiography?' There was a pause and he responded, 'We are feeling waggish this morning.' Not that he refrained from teasing me. When I gave the wrong directions in the car, for instance, he told me I was a 'fearful know all'.

On the April weekend in 1976 I drove down from London with Woodrow on Saturday morning. This was the beginning of jolly escapades. We stopped at Hungerford to buy things to eat. The baker was called Wyatt's, so Woodrow hailed the shopkeeper as a cousin. Then on to the grocers. This was a full scale performance with Woodrow complaining about the expense of everything and that he couldn't afford the potatoes, nor the cabbage. When it came to paying he plunged a hand into his pockets and scattered loose bundles of £10 notes, dollars and Italian million lire bills over the counter and floor. The grocer extracted about 6 pence and returned the rest. On Saturday afternoon, we visited Rowdeforde House where Matthew Digby Wyatt had been born and which is now a school. We just walked in and wandered into all the rooms discoursing on the quality of the cornices and chimney-pieces. As we came down into the hall again, the Head Master's wife met us. We pretended to have just come in. I dread to think what she might have said if she had found us prowling round the girls' dormitories. She struck me as mad, certainly jittery, and started going on about ghosts (always a bore). I'm surprised she did not faint on finding two strange men in her front hall.

We also mopped up various Wiltshire works of T.H. Wyatt, including the rectory at Collingbourne Ducis which I thought might be by him but in fact is not. It is a typical gaunt, Victorian, brick, muscular Gothic structure with plate glass windows. All was very dilapidated with laurels gone wild and bits of junk lying about. We peered through the windows—one of the rooms was full of carpentry equipment. We walked round the back, making loud remarks about the architectural de-merits of the building and its dilapidated condition, to find all the family staring at us from the kitchen window. We waved and they let us in through the back door. They didn't seem surprised to find us trespassing in their garden. We asked them if they knew who the architect was. 'Oh yes, they replied, 'G.E. Street prepared plans but they weren't executed and the house was built to a design by Ingelowe, a local man.'

I was nonplussed by this as I didn't expect the rustic owners of an obscure dilapidated rectory to have such information at their fingertips. He turned out to be Arthur Popham's son (the great keeper of drawings at the British Museum). They were very jolly and not at all put out by our impertinent behaviour; he gave us coffee. Woodrow always had a good technique. He trespassed shamelessly. Then when the umbrageous owner popped up to demand 'what do you think you are doing?' and asked the inevitable question, 'Who are you?', he said 'Woodrow Wyatt', whom they all remembered from some 1960s television programme when he had started Panorama with Richard Dimbleby. It always worked. They switched on smiles in mid-flight, becoming sycophantic or just nice, and asked us in for a drink.

There was a delightful ongoing feud between Woodrow and his neighbours the Sykes, who lived in the real house at Conock. Woodrow referred to theirs as 'the new manor'. They called his 'that little glebe house' and thought it flash and over-heated, which it was. The *Victoria County History* volume had just been published and proved that the Sykes house was early 18th century (older than Woodrow's) and built on the site of a medieval manor. Woodrow described the Sykes' house as a freezing uncomfortable mess. I thought it the acme of intelligent, informed, civilisation—with its grand-shabby mix of good things, dogs and broken croquet mallets. They had a splendid outdoor Gothic privy which they called the 'Grotto Loo'. I wonder if it is still there. The house has subsequently changed hands and been shampooed with New Money like so many once charming Wiltshire houses.

As cooks go, George, the poofy cook, went. He was replaced for Easter by a Hungarian couple who didn't speak a word of English. All conversation had to be through Verushka's mother who acted as interpreter. Thus, if breakfast arrived cold, you had to ring her in the cottage to find out how to say, 'can this be warmed up, please,' in Hungarian. Woodrow spoke to them in the Anglo-Italian he used at their Tuscan villa: 'Grazie Mille', he bellowed when they brought a dish of boiling, steaming goulash, 'Bene, bene.' They retreated looking bemused. Being served the goulash, I made a mess of things and ladled it all into the lap of Nicholas Banszky (Woodrow's stepson), sitting next to me. His mother Verushka said laconically, 'Do not move, I don't want it on the seat cover.'

On a subsequent weekend in May 1976, we visited Longleat to see the house (Wyatville) and then had tea with Lord Bath. The visit was memorable. Christopher Thynne, who looked after the house in his father's time, showed us round. We made a sensational procession when we descended from the roof and down the Grand Staircase: Henry Bath sniffing snuff and waving a spotty red hanky, a huge mastiff called Leo, Woodrow smoking a large cigar and booming Wyatville's merits as if he were still alive and he was recommending his employment to add a new wing; the rest of us trailing behind looking surplus.

We were showered with throw-away remarks. 'There are no good pictures here. Oh that? That is by Titian.' Or, when looking down from the roof over the park and spreading outbuildings: 'That is where the public disport themselves,' with a lordly wave towards the stables. 'That is the car park over there. I've planted it with lime trees. Apparently they are unsuitable and drip sticky stuff all over the cars—perhaps I should open a car cleaning place at the exit.' 'NO! That is not my banner. It is my son's flag of Wessex. Ridiculous!'

The library is fabulous—about 60,000 volumes including Caxtons. It is a great privilege to turn the pages of the first book printed in English—Caxton's *History of Troy*—in this handsome place. The most pleasant room in the house is Bishop Ken's Library like the inside of a Georgian warship admiral's cabin which runs round two sides of the building on the second floor at the top. It was full of Hitleriana, half-smoked Churchillian cigar ends and other miscellaneous relics and goodies collected by Henry Bath—very different from a dull, academic library.

Henry Bath lived at Job's Mill, a pretty little house on the estate to which we retired. We began by drinking strong India tea out of Woolworth's mugs but soon moved on to vintage champagne from

French Empire tulip-shaped glasses. Henry loved Longleat with an infectious passion which Woodrow drew out with his good-natured badinage. He saved the house and estate in the difficult post-war years. Under the eccentric veneer and rampant tourism it remains an impressively well-preserved and well run place today.

On another occasion in September 1976 we went from Conock to Anne Fleming's at Sevenhampton for Sunday lunch. The house is a neo-Georgian reconstruction—the result of drastic curtailment of an old house. I said politely how pretty it was. Mrs Fleming retorted that the best description of her house was in Evelyn Waugh's *Diary*. When I looked it up later, the relevant passage read 'Nothing had prepared us for the full horror of Anne's edifice ...' The other guests in 1976 included Douglas Hurd, Peter Quennell (Editor of *History Today*) and somebody called Crispin from the Foreign Office. Much talk about contemporary Heathgate politics in which I was not interested. Douglas Hurd and Peter Quennell, however, discoursed amusingly on Heath's 'involuntary ungraciousness', citing as an example his having lunch at ..., the telephone rang for Heath and Octavian, the son, took him to the nearest one, in the butler's pantry, 'apologising' with easy Etonian manners to the Prime Minister for its 'unsuitability', to which Heath snapped: 'It's not your fault. You can't help it!' Hurd also described the Prime Minister's hospitality at Chequers: 'The food is too bad and the wine too good.'

On my way back to London in the car, Woodrow chatted about this and that; he said that Tom Driberg bought Bradwell Lodge, a desirable eighteenth century house in Essex, for £3,000 which he received as compensation for a traffic accident just before the War when he was knocked over by a car in Piccadilly and broke a limb. 'He never had any money of his own.' The journey up to London was better than coming down, when we had a haunch of venison in the boot. This was a present to Woodrow from the Ranger of the Royal Parks (Richmond). It stank to high heaven and not all the cigar smoke could blot it out. I felt sea-green on arrival at Conock. Woodrow was frightfully proud of this almost royal gift, and a timid suggestion that it might be a 'bit off' was swept aside. When the cook unwrapped it, however, it was not merely 'high' but crawling with huge maggots. It was promptly buried by Gunthorpe in the garden. What a relief. I had not been looking forward to Saturday dinner.

Sometimes I stayed at Conock on my own to get on with writing 'in peace', at Woodrow's kind suggestion. Peaceful except for the weekday sound of heavy artillery gunfire from tank training on Salisbury Plain. One of the last family weekends there was in May 1977, a year after the maggoty venison. Nicholas and his (then) new wife, Eve, were also staying. On Saturday, Simon Weinstock and others came to dinner. Afterwards we played Scrabble. Simon won by about 100 points. This was a return match. When we previously went to the Weinstocks house, a James Wyatt masterpiece, Bowden Park near Lacock, Arnold Weinstock had treated us there to a lavish lunch starting with a huge pot of caviar, 'a present from the Shah'.

Woodrow got cross on that last visit to Conock in 1977. Verushka was sitting smoking in the drawing room, cool as an icicle, while he raged about the lack of arrangements for lunch and her late arrival from London (she had come on after the rest of us). 'I wish you wouldn't make such an exhibition of yourself,' he yelled and stomped out of the room. This followed a heated game of croquet, the announcement that there was only an omelette and the loss of the cellar keys—so there was to be no drink either—and a summons to court on Nicholas's behalf as the latter had failed to pay a traffic fine while away on honeymoon. Thank God, I'd stayed out of all this and didn't play either tennis or croquet. If you are not very good at something it always pays to pretend that you can't do it at all, rather than mucking in and getting in everybody's way. I slunk off and wrote in my room.

I finished the Wyatts that summer, though it was not published until the beginning of 1980 as OUP with its Victorian technology still took up to a couple of years to produce a book, with two stages of proofs and preparing an index. *The Wyatts* was the only one of my books where I prepared the index myself. I found the task so horrific that in all subsequent works, I have paid for a professional indexer.

Woodrow was brilliant at arranging visits to inaccessible places. For instance, much later when I said in the 1980s I would love to see Sir Matthew Digby Wyatt's Durbar Court in the former India Office which had been absorbed into the Foreign Office after Independence, and had recently been restored, Woodrow just rang the Foreign Secretary and all was arranged. Geoffrey Howe showed us round personally, in between negotiating rapprochement with Gorbachev and the Warsaw Pact countries and drafting the Sino-British agreement over the future of Hong Kong. He also gave us a cup of tea.

The complete Wyatt text was handed to the Press in September 1977. I subsequently went up to Oxford to make some corrections to the typescript and hand over Patrick Lichfield's and Geoffrey's last batch of photographs, and Woodrow's Foreword which he had kindly contributed and which I had collected from Cavendish Avenue. At the porter's lodge in Walton Street I had my moment. 'You don't work here?' 'No, I am an author.' A first book is, I imagine, like a first baby; subsequent works do not provide the same innocent thrill. Through my day job for the GLC Historic Buildings Committee, I was able to organise the erection of a Blue Plaque to T.H. Wyatt on his house in Bloomsbury, next to the British Museum, and for the launch of the book Woodrow unveiled the plaque there to his ancestor. Susan Boyd, the novelist William Boyd's wife was then publicity girl at OUP in charge of the party and the reviews. William was my contemporary. He had been at Gordonstoun when I was at Fort Augustus, at Glasgow when I was at St Andrews, and Oxford when I was at Oxford. Susan Boyd was the most efficient person I encountered at OUP, perhaps because she is Scottish, and she worked with me on subsequent books, notably my history of the Norfolks. Nevertheless, various small hitches occurred in the Wyatt arrangements. The man who was doing the catering broke his neck, for instance. And I forgot to send invitations for the plaque unveiling to a host of GLC grandees, but fortunately my colleague Frank Kelsall reminded me and we were able to do it just in time.

I owed Woodrow a great debt for his help with this book. Not only had he provided me a consultancy fee for years while researching it, provided wonderful hospitality, and poured the contents of his spectacular wine cellar down my gullet, but also paid Patrick Lichfield for the photographs and OUP for all the additional colour printing. Without his generosity and enthusiasm it would have been a lesser book and the writing less fun. I am still proud of this, my first serious work.

I only wish I had had more room for amusing anecdotes. I've always loved, for example, Georgiana Fullerton's description of her first grown-up dinner at Chatsworth in 1830. 'The night we arrived I sat at dinner by a grey-haired gentleman whose name I did not know. He asked me if I admired the new wing which had just been added to the house. I answered that I thought the house must have had a better effect without it ... I was horrified to find that the gentleman was Sir Jeffry Wyatville who had designed the said wing.'

The Unveiling of the Blue Plaque at Great Russell Street went off well and afterwards there was a party inside the house in Wyatt's drawing room, thanks to the Bedford Estate (who own it), on 24 January 1980. Bucks Fizz and decent eats were provided. Trevor-Roper, and friends, patrons and colleagues came along. Woodrow made a funny speech about T.H. Wyatt's lunatic asylums, and the Office of Works sending him two large stone balls from Old Knightsbridge Barracks [T.H. Wyatt] when he objected to its being demolished. Godfrey Barker (the art critic of the *Evening Standard)* turned to me and muttered *sotto voce*: 'Thank God the hereditary talent for architecture has died out or just think of the *folies de grandeur* which Woodrow might have designed.'

The Wyatts was the beginning of my writing career which has been a major strand of my life, and provided a useful occupation during interminable train journeys. The train from London

Above: Blue Plaque to Thomas Henry Wyatt, in Great Russell Street. Unveiled by Woodrow Wyatt at the publication party for JMR's The Wyatts, An Architectural Dynasty.*1978.*

to Lancashire (250 miles) takes just under two and a half hours, and my weekly visit to Sussex (60 miles) takes an hour and a half, even without delays. Generally, trains provide a detached space where one can concentrate, often, surprisingly, in peace. Although I do not smoke (put off by my father who smoked sixty a day until he was eighty), I used to travel in the Second Class smoking carriage as it was the quietest place, and a child-free zone. Once, when for some reason, I was in a First Class carriage at Euston and I had just got all my notes and writing paper arranged in front of me on the table, a young couple whom I did not know came in with their two boisterous babies, and sat down in the seats next to me, a terrible intrusion and disturbance. I glared at them. After a pause he said mildly, 'You are making my wife feel uncomfortable.' To which I replied, 'Oh Good! I am president of the King Herod Society and I loathe babies! It is very selfish to bring them into a First Class carriage where people want to work in peace. Why can't their nanny take them into Third Class ...' He put his head in his hands, she looked murderous. I gathered up my things and stomped off, hissing, to the adjoining carriage. The next day at a meeting in Kendal our Lord-Lieutenant smilingly said to me, 'Oh, I hear you met my grandchildren yesterday ...'!

Generally, trains provide a good time to sort the week's research notes from libraries in London and county record offices, and to write them up. Most of my books have been about architectural history, but I have also written about heraldry, travel, and the odd biography, including that of Cardinal Consalvi. He was Vatican Secretary of State at the Congress of Vienna, which provided me with the excuse to spend some weeks in Rome researching in the *Archivio Segreto* in the Vatican and in the archives of the *Propaganda Fidei* in a palace designed by Bernini *and* Borromini, while staying at the English College. (Hotels do not always provide writing tables with reading lamps, an essential amenity.)

Through Alexandra Artley, when we were working together on the *New Georgian Handbook*, I met Dieter Klein, a German who lived in Kensington. He became my literary agent until his death. He had a knack of placing my books and securing publishers for agreeable subjects that I wanted to write about. After the Wyatts, I wrote the history of the *Dukes of Norfolk* and a history of *Georgian Model Farms* for OUP. They also commissioned me to write the *Oxford Guide to Heraldry* which I did jointly with my fellow Lancastrian then Somerset Herald of Arms and now Garter King of Arms, Thomas Woodcock. It did better than architecture, selling over 30,000 copies and went into paperback.

Through Dieter, however, I secured a regular succession of books for different publishers on reasonably popular, well-illustrated subjects—*Royal Residences, The English Country Estate, The English Country House at War, Treasures of English Churches,* and similar subjects. Perhaps the most successful in one sense was the *Latest Country Houses* published in 1983 by Bodley Head which I initiated as a joke. Clive Aslet had written an excellent book—he is a very good writer (a pupil of Watkin's at Cambridge)—about Edwardian Arts & Crafts and inter-wars houses in both England and America, finishing in 1939. His publishers called it *The Last*

Country Houses. In my review in the *Spectator*, I pointed out that a large number of proper country houses had been built in Britain since 1947. To my surprise, this led to a commission from David Machin at Bodley Head to write *The Latest Country Houses*, about new houses constructed between the 1940s and 1980. They were a social and architectural phenomenon that was then little known; the survival of the landed estate and the continuation of the classical architectural tradition having been 'Snopaked' out of 'our island story'.

The hard-back edition sold out and the book went into paper back, so it was successful as a publication, but led to me being sued for libel by an ageing modernist architect called Stephen Gardiner, who did not like my description of a house he had designed. He was architectural critic of the *Sunday Times* and used their lawyers to prosecute his case against a young writer, which I still think was a case of ungentlemanly and asymmetric warfare. I ignored the hail of pompous lawyers' missives, until the WRIT arrived! The libel case caused me a great deal of stress at a difficult moment. It led to a painful attack of pancreatitis which the doctors feared might be cancer. Fortunately it wasn't and I am always grateful to the doctors at Barts who were professional and sympathetic, as well as the students there, for Barts is a teaching hospital and my case was a teaching aid. I always remember a student doctor telling me quietly before any official results came through, that the tests were fine and that it was *not* cancer. Until then it had never crossed my mind that it might be, but I was touched that he thought I might be desperately worried, and out of kindness had wanted to reassure me. My publisher, David Machin at Bodley Head behaved like a gentleman. Unlike me, BH was insured, and paid Gardiner off. The Sun Alliance smiled on the just.

Despite this incident, on the whole my writing career has not backfired against me personally, but I do seem to have been bad news for a succession of publishers. I have only to appear on the doormat of a publishing house, for the firm to go bankrupt, the editors and staff to be sacked, or some other plague of Egypt to smite them. Hardly any of the firms I have written for over the years still exist in the same form. MacDonald Futura which published *Royal Residences* were taken over by Robert Maxwell, the 'bouncing Czech', hardly before the ink was dry on the contract and all the staff left. Burke's Peerage (*Country Houses of the North West*) and Sinclair Stevenson (*Treasures of English Churches*) went bankrupt, while Aurum Press (*The Destruction of the English Country Estate, Regency Country Houses* and *The Country House at War*) was taken over by an investment syndicate and my excellent editor made redundant; and I do not feel that sales of *Georgian Model Farms* or *Cardinal Consalvi* can have done much for the profits of OUP or Bodley Head, nor repaid my editors' kindness and faith in my recherché chosen subjects. Even *James Wyatt*, eventually published by Yale University Press in 2013, was followed immediately by the termination of the employment there of my excellent supportive editor, Sally Salveson. Publishing, like most aspects of the British economy which I have encountered over the last forty years, has been far from successful, but at least my books came out before their midwives sank below the waves.

4
The 'Last Enchantments'

ARUNDEL CASTLE has been a significant and absorbing part of life for over forty years, with general oversight of the library, archives, art collection and the historic aspects. In that time, four butlers, six comptrollers, three ducal secretaries, three head gardeners have come and gone, and there has been a complete changeover of lodge-keepers, security men, housemaids, housemen, groundsmen, all the household and the Opening Staff, even though some of them continued into their eighties. On first visits in the 1970s, one encountered astonishing links with the past. Ted Puttock, the Head Lodge Keeper had started out before the War as Hall Boy at Norfolk House in St James's Square (demolished in 1938). The old cook was a Belgian refugee from the First World War. The 15th Duke of Norfolk had been chairman of the Belgian Refugee Committee in 1914 and several Belgians came to Arundel. Mrs Wallop stayed until her death in the 1980s. I feel that I am myself now a Gothic fixture, a labelstop, a lierne, a corbel or possibly a gargoyle. I was appointed Librarian on Guy Fawkes Day 1978; in fact a bit earlier in the autumn of that year but it seemed a good joke to formalise it from the 5th November: 'Remember, remember, the 5th of November.' I first visited the castle in April 1976, so have known it now for 45 years, an eternity.

The role of Librarian to the Duke of Norfolk has distinguished scholarly predecessors. The first was Francis Junius (1591-1677) who was Librarian to the 14th (Collector) Earl of Arundel, (the dukedom was under attainder from the execution of the 4th Duke of Norfolk in 1577 for attempting to marry Mary Queen of Scots, the Catholic heir to the throne, until the Restoration of Charles II in 1660.) Junius was born in Heidelberg and was the first serious scholar of the early

JMR at Arundel Castle, 1979, with the Coade Stone Norfolk Lion originally erected by the 12th Duke of Norfolk on the Shoreham Suspension Bridge in 1826.

Anglo-Saxon and German languages and author of *De Pictura Veterum.* The latter was commissioned by the Collector Earl, and became the basis of classical art studies in the 18th century. Junius was appointed in 1620, but left England in 1642 for the Low Countries, travelling with his aged employer (who died in Padua) and Alatheia Countess of Arundel (who died in Antwerp), as the Civil War overwhelmed Charles I's Court and its culture. Like Pope Gregory VII, Lord Arundel could have said, 'I have loved beauty and truth, therefore I die in exile.' Junius returned to England after the Restoration but not to the Norfolk's employ, gravitating to Oxford and dying at Windsor. He is buried in St George's Chapel, at Windsor Castle.

In the late 17th and 18th centuries when the Norfolk Howards remained recusant Catholics their chaplains, who were scholarly Jesuits and Benedictines, served as librarians. At both Norfolk House and Arundel Castle in the 18th century, the libraries adjoined the priest's apartment. The most interesting of the clerical librarians was the Revd Alban Butler (1710-1773) appointed in 1749. He was author of the multi-volumed *Lives of the Fathers, Martyrs and Other Principal Saints* (1756-9). This work still provides much of the information on the subject for Wikipedia which describes it as 'part of the knowledge base of civilization as we know it'. Butler received a grudging compliment from Edward Gibbon: 'The sense is the author's own. The superstition is that of his religion.'

Charles, 11th Duke conformed to the Established Church in 1780 as Earl of Surrey in order to contest an election in Carlisle against the nominee of the Tory Earl of Lonsdale, son-in-law of the unpopular Lord Bute. He won, and became a strong Foxite Whig and heavy drinker. When taking the Anglican Communion (for the first and last time), he is supposed to have exclaimed 'By God, it's port.' George III was not taken in, and when the Duke and other more-or-less Catholics in the Society of Antiquaries blackballed the architect James Wyatt 'the Destroyer', the King referred to it jokingly as 'a Popish Plot.' (Wyatt with royal support, got in at the next election). Having to a degree lapsed from his hereditary religion, the Duke moved the chapel and the priest out of the castle to the outbuildings but continued to maintain both. He felt nevertheless he could not use the Catholic Priest as his librarian and employed a succession of independent scholars including James Dallaway, appointed the Earl Marshal's Secretary, who wrote the standard *History of the Western Division of Sussex*. The duke also used the historical and archive skills of his cousin Henry Howard of Corby, who had been an officer in the Empress Maria Teresa's Austrian army. Henry Howard catalogued the medieval deeds then stored at Norfolk House and wrote the *Memorials of the Howard Family*.

The 11th Duke, despite his reputation as a drunkard and father of at least six illegitimate children, was a well-educated product of the Enlightenment, an effective man of business who enlarged and re-organised the estates. He pioneered in the 1780s that evergreen English institution, allotment gardens, for his tenants in Sheffield so that they could grow their own vegetables. Above all, he was an enthusiastic bibliophile who subscribed contemporaneously to Diderot's *Encyclopédie* and added the greatest treasures to the library, including an (unwashed, unlike all those in America) First Folio of Shakespeare and a magnificent 15th century Burgundian illuminated manuscript of the Golden Legend by the Master of Metz. He built the present library (a room 110 feet long) at Arundel to his own design, out of mahogany which he had bought wholesale as logs in London Docks, and had carved by his own workmen John Teasdale, father and son.

The 'Drunken Duke's' successor was a man of different stamp and a strong Catholic. He immediately appointed a learned Catholic priest to both posts, chaplain and librarian. The Revd Canon Mark Aloysius Tierney F.S.A. (1775-1862) was librarian and chaplain to three successive Dukes of Norfolk from the 1820s to 1862. He wrote the definitive *History of Arundel* and was the longest incumbent in the post. The 15th Duke employed professional archivists in the later 19th century, who catalogued the archives in the Muniment Room at Norfolk House. In 1904 the Duke appointed Richard Wilton, an Oxford MA, who had been Anglican rector at Everingham in the East Riding of Yorkshire but became a Catholic, so lost his job. The Duke provided him with new employment. Wilton was also secretary to the Catholic Records Society which published much original source material of considerable use to historians. His main achievement as Librarian was to pack up the historical archives including deeds dating from the 12th century, when Norfolk House was sold in 1938 and move them to Arundel. In 1978 many were still wrapped in 1930s brown paper parcels annotated with their subject and reference number in R.C. Wilton's hand, and stored on wooden shelves made of old champagne cases which had been used to transport them before the outbreak of War.

Wilton died in 1947. During the War the castle and much of the estate were requisitioned for five years by the army. The archives were left safe and undisturbed in the basement. The library was locked and used to store furniture and paintings decanted from the other main rooms. Moths spent a well-fed time there feasting on the thick Victorian textiles, some of which, like the library curtains, had to be copied and replaced in the 1980s and1990s when the main rooms were restored to Victorian splendour as part of a comprehensive resuscitation scheme for the interior of the castle.

After the War the house reopened to the public in 1947, and in 1950, Dr Francis Steer, then the Sussex county archivist, was appointed Librarian to the Duke of Norfolk and started to sort, shelve and catalogue the archives. He was a pluralist serving also as Archivist to the College of Arms, New College, Oxford, and Chichester Cathedral, as well as being Maltravers Herald Extra Ordinary. He died in the summer of 1978 and I succeeded him the same year. The first thing to say is that I am not a professional librarian nor an archivist, but a historian and antiquary, like most of my predecessors. As for the latter, I was elected young to the Society of Antiquaries, on 1 March 1979, which was unusual for that body, predominantly of grey-haired archaeologists, the 'barrow boys' as they were nicknamed by Clive Wainwright of the Victoria & Albert Museum.

So how did the Arundel Castle involvement arise? It was a matter of chance, acquaintance and sideways inheritance. Miles, the 17th Duke of Norfolk (1915-2002) inherited from a cousin in April 1975, and I knew him before. I remember being astonished by the *Evening Standard* headlines seen in a London street: Earl Marshal dies, 'the heir is a distant cousin, a retired Major-General', with a photograph of Miles. He had of course known since the 1950s that he and his eldest son would succeed one day, but it had not loomed large in his life. Until his inheritance Miles had not been to Arundel since the War, and that visit had not been for family reasons. In June 1940 when the Grenadiers were evacuated to Sussex from Dunkirk they had been put in a temporary tented camp in the park at Arundel. Bernard Norfolk had also been evacuated from Dunkirk, and been invalided out of the army becoming Principal Parliamentary Secretary for Agriculture in the House of Lords. He invited the evacuated officers to dinner in the Smoking Room at the castle.

Bernard Norfolk knew his younger cousin from children's Christmas parties at Norfolk House in the 1920s and 1930s, but their paths had increasingly diverged, Miles following the career of a professional soldier. After a 'good war' with service in Italy and Germany, and an MC, ending in command of BRIXMS in Berlin, he had commanded the King's African Rifles in Kenya in 1963 where he promoted black African officers (including Idi Amin) prior to Independence. He then served as Commander of the First Division of the British Army of the Rhine from 1963 to 1965.

Apart from his official and civic duties, Bernard was occupied with horses and cricket, being the Queen's Representative at Ascot for twenty-seven years and Senior Steward of the Jockey Club as well as a breeder and trainer. He was involved in cricket as the President of the MCC, and manager of the English test tour to Australia and New Zealand in 1962-3. The players were a bit worried what they should call him. 'Oh don't bother with Your Grace,' was the response 'Just call me Earl Marshal', which recalls Lord Chetwode's direction to his son-in-law John Betjeman: 'Don't stand on formality, call me Field Marshal'. Miles had no interest in either horses or cricket, and had his own estates in Yorkshire and Lancashire which had nothing to do with the Howards but came through his mother Mona Stapleton who had inherited the Beaumont barony, a medieval title in fee which could pass through the female line, at the age of one when her father died in a shooting accident.

When I first met Miles in the early 1970s he had succeeded his mother as Lord Beaumont. When his father, Lord Howard of Glossop died, he never used that title as he did not want to change his name too many times. He realised that he would also inherit in due course the premier dukedom, the premier earldom and two other Earldoms, five more baronies, and the role of Earl Marshal which is an hereditary title as well as one of the Great Offices of State, introduced by the Normans after the model of Charlemagne's Court. When giving prizes at prep schools after his great inheritance, he used to amuse the school children by saying 'I have 10 seats in the House of Lords but only one bottom to put in them.' He was a man of enormous charm and military directness. He used to say 'Call me Miles' to complete strangers and some did: 'Call-me-Miles.' His soldiers nicknamed him Kilometres. 'Here comes fucking Kilometres', he would hear them mutter as he passed.

Despite his modesty, he was proud of his family and keen on history which he had read at Christ Church, Oxford, under Noel Myers, and like many of his ancestors he was especially interested in the history of the Howards and Arundel.

My introduction to Miles when he was Lord Beaumont, came through St Benet's Hall at Oxford. Two of Miles's nephews there, Tom and Harry Fitzalan Howard, became friends as did Fr James Forbes, the Master of that Benedictine House. Fr James had been at school at Ampleforth with Miles, and they remained friends partly because of their shared historical interests; though one of them had become a monk and the other a soldier. Fr James, though devout and sincere, was not everyone's idea of a simple monk, as he was very social and interested in old buildings and 'Things'. He spent much time out of the abbey staying in country houses, including annual Christmases at Carlton Towers, the Beaumont seat near Selby in the old West Riding.

I came to stay regularly at Carlton too. When it was opened to the public in 1976, as a condition of a Historic Buildings Council grant for the roof, I helped Miranda, Miles's youngest sister (there were eight siblings and all their Christian names began with M), arrange the place to show to the public. We had great fun moving furniture around, ordering druggets and ropes, and replacement wallpaper and fabrics from Watts, and bringing things out of store. We found the Gothic revival fire dogs and fire irons designed by J.F. Bentley for the chimney-pieces in the state rooms in boxes in the basement. They were wrapped in 1939 newspaper in which they had been packed away at the beginning of the War when the house was converted to a military hospital.

After the War the big rooms were closed except for a September house party for Doncaster Races and the annual Hunt Ball for the York and Ainsty, so there had never been any reason to reinstate all the Victoriana until we did. It was thrilling, as was going to the bank at Selby and choosing silver for display in the dining room: wine coolers by Paul Storr, and German gilt tankards. Some was later sold, but some silver was kept and is more seen now as the younger generation have put in a modern kitchen, restored the Georgian dining room, and use the silver. In the 1970s, apart from the drinks table on a marble slab behind the colonnade at one end, the dining room was not used and the furniture was kept under dust covers; while the dark green paint on the walls survived from the post-war rehabilitation in 1947 after use as the hospital staff room.

If your idea of a country house is a rosy, symmetrical Queen Anne, or Georgian dream, Carlton may not be for you. Evelyn Waugh described it in his diary in July 1939: 'First sight of the house is staggering, concrete faced, ivy-grown, 1870-early-Tudor bristling with gargoyles, heraldic animals carrying fully emblazoned banners, coroneted cyphers; an orgy of heraldry ... Closer inspection, however, reveals many charms.' That was exactly my first impression in the early-1970s. I loved it: the eccentric individuality, the quality of the craftsmanship in the refined Gothic state rooms by J.F. Bentley (architect of Westminster Cathedral), the unexpected surviving Georgian interiors, the extraordinary silhouette with three jagged towers and battlements rising over the flat park and the surrounding fen landscape. The fields of black soil were criss-crossed with muddy river estuaries, dykes and canals, and the distant silhouettes of 1960s and 1970s concrete cooling towers of the electric power stations Drax, Barnby Don, Eggborough, Ferrybridge and other places with resonant Viking names, made an extraordinary contrast to the Victorian romanticism of the house. Some might have thought the cooling towers representatives of 'progress' and a 'modern' threat, but in fact the coal-fired power stations (and the coal mines) have largely gone, while the extraordinary house and the well-farmed estate continue.

Staying at Carlton was jolly and relaxed, and there was always something to do, not boring things like tennis, but browsing in the undisturbed eighteenth century library, finding boxes of old drawings and plans. There was lots of 'out-doors', going with Rowland the keeper in his Land Rover round the fields at night, talking about the Middle Ages, as well as wild life. Miles liked to set a party to work, cutting down a tree in the garden on a Sunday between Mass and lunch, or stripping ivy off a Gothick folly, or memorably for me, up a ladder repainting the Beaumont arms on the Bentley-designed cottages in the village where the estate painter had given the Errington quartering a yellow touch up. We repainted it in the correct azure and argent, prior to a visit from Garter King of Arms who would have been shocked by such a solecism on a property of the Earl Marshal.

Or there was the day at dinner in 1978 when the Duke was given a note at table saying a new Pope had been elected. The *News of the World* had just rung and would like His Grace's views? We had no idea in Yorkshire that there *was* a new Pope. Miles had to ring the Papal Nuncio in London to find out who it was; John Paul I who only reigned for 33 days. The Earl Marshal represented the Queen at both his enthronement, and his funeral, and then the enthronement of the Polish Pope, John Paul II. On these occasions, ricocheting backwards and forwards to Rome, Miles stayed at the English College. One of his sisters remarked, 'I hope they didn't bother to change the sheets.'

John Paul II was a 'good thing' from the start, the Cardinal Archbishop of Cracow, doughty enemy of Communism, and representative of 'old Europe'. He was charming with a sense of humour. When he visited England in 1982, the Order of Malta provided ceremonial staff for his Mass at Westminster Cathedral and to line the staircase in Archbishops House. As the Pope came down the stairs where I was standing on the half landing, he stopped and said to me in English, with a laugh,'I had no idea the Knights of Malta were so young', and passed on followed by a train of monsignors.

In the 1960s and 1970s country houses were still recovering from the War, and were generally kept going on a shoe-string. Frugality and Spartan restraint prevailed. Looking back now from warm houses, with numerous bathrooms and every modern facility to those days, with scuffed but clean old paint, threadbare carpets, the few cast iron baths supported on claw feet in the middle of bleak linoleum floors, the one-bar electric fires, it all seems a world away. It took fifty years for British houses to recover from the Second World War, even if they were not demolished outright. I appreciated houses in their poetic decline, before Mrs Thatcher's economic revolution. I liked the contrasts and eccentricity; 'frayed charm' mitigating the 'austere splendour of riches'. It was more subtle and enchanting than mere opulence. In my view expensive things need to be faded and worn to be beautiful. It was a world of Gucci shoes and Marks & Spencer shirts, of Lancashire hot pot and silver gilt coasters, of coroneted writing paper and cyphered towels, with worn out rugs and frayed curtains and pervading cold, Asprey's and Floris, and coal tar soap and Bronco lavatory paper.

Hindsight may be tinged by youthful acquaintance with houses in Scotland where Spartan frugality was cultivated for its own sake, and was responsible for admirable traits of the Northern British Character, now all mumsied and feminised away. You have to be careful criticising a Scotsman today, not because he will punch you in the face as of yore, but because he may burst into tears or make a whingeing complaint to Social Services.

Carlton was not in Scotland, but it shared some of the same characteristics, being the northern home of a military family. Miles's father, who had been partly brought up at Mount Stuart in Scotland by his Aunt Bute (wife of the 3rd Marquess, protean patron of Burges and Gothic architecture), had fought in the Lovat

Scouts in the First World War and taken part at Gallipoli where many of the Highland soldiers died of dysentery because, used to a diet of oatmeal porridge and herrings, they couldn't cope with army rations and were poisoned by the tinned bully beef. Miles and his brothers served in the Grenadiers and the Scots Guards. Oliver Millar, keeper of The Queen's pictures, who knew and admired them, said, 'They are Arthurian figures, combining charm, gentleness and Christian chivalry with military toughness and efficiency.' Miles called the effective combination of himself and his three brothers 'The Thin Red Line', as in the British Infantry.

I admired the world of country houses as I knew them when a teenager, their picturesque decay and character-forming austerity. Carlton was a continuation of that world and still run on a tight budget after Lady Beaumont died in the early 1970s. The house was only opened up by Miles for Christmas parties, and occasional weekends, especially his birthday week in June when it was always hot weather. Because the dining room was so far away from the kitchen, they had converted the Still Room downstairs in the basement to a new dining room. This created an eccentric effect, as you walked for miles down a bleak and dark, stone-floored passage and through a door into a newly wallpapered room with the mahogany furniture previously in the London house, convenient and close to the kitchen, but oddly unexpected.

In the summer of 1978, three years after Miles succeeded his cousin Bernard as Duke of Norfolk, the old Librarian at Arundel Castle, Dr Francis Steer, died. I went to his memorial service at Chichester Cathedral though we had not got on very well, as unbeknown to me he had had a scholar's spat with Howard Colvin, and disapproved of me at one remove as a Colvin pupil! So he had made no effort to involve me at the castle or to show me much though he knew that such things would have interested me.

Now he was dead, Miles said to me 'You are keen on history, would you like to take it on?' I said I had a full-time job in London, working for the GLC Historic Buildings Committee. (I was to be the only person in the 1980s who worked for 'Red Ken' Livingstone and the Earl Marshal.) He replied 'that doesn't matter, come down when you feel like it. There is a marvellous person in the town here, Sara, the sister of Fr Benet Perceval and married to a retired naval officer, she would be happy to come in a couple of days a week and look after the researchers.' So Sara and I worked together harmoniously for over thirty years, later with professional archivists especially Heather Warne who carried on the archive cataloguing, a Forth Bridge job that seems to be eternal.

At first I used to go down to the castle for odd days, often Saturdays, and set myself the task of replacing the makeshift shelves made of wooden champagne cases in the muniment tower with purpose-made Dexian steel shelves and proper plan chests, and 'stock-taking' the books, checking the 1904 Hatchards catalogue, sitting on the floor in the library leafing through the leather bound volumes. A regular question from visitors to country houses when confronted with miles of shelves and gold tooled bindings is 'Does anybody read these books?' the answer is 'Yes'. I can go further than that, and while not claiming to have read all the books, I can say I have looked at every single book on the shelves in the historic library, about 10,000 of the total of around 20,000 in the castle, and jolly interesting they were too, as many of them contained annotations and occasional notes and letters from historic figures.

The immediate point of my job was to write a new family history to mark the 500th anniversary of the Norfolk dukedom in 1983, a volume that OUP agreed to publish, with the same editorial team, and Susan Boyd for publicity, as for the Wyatts. The quincentenial history took up most of my immediate efforts. The completed book *The Dukes of Norfolk* was published by OUP in 1983. It received more reviews than any other book I have written, and Christina Foyle gave one of her literary lunches at the Grosvenor Hotel, at which Enoch Powell and I gave speeches.

The history formed part of the wider celebrations of the ducal quincentenary that summer. John Howard, a Yorkist supporter in East Anglia had been created 1st Duke of Norfolk (of his family) on 28 June 1483 by Richard III. Miles (17th Duke) organised a party in London on the same day in 1983, beginning with an ecumenical service at the Tower of London, followed by dinner at the Fishmongers, of which he was Renter Warden that year. Two hundred and fifty guests attended, of whom two hundred were members of the Howard family, including the titled heads of the different branches—Carlisle, Suffolk, Penrith. The quincentenary took place at the Royal Chapel of St Peter ad Vincula in the Tower where the 4th Duke had been buried after his execution in 1572.

The service was presided over by Cardinal Basil Hume (Archbishop of Westminster), Archbishop Bruno Heim (Papal Nuncio), Bishop Cormack Murphy O'Connor, (Bishop of Arundel and Brighton), Robert Runcie (Archbishop of Canterbury), with his chaplain Richard Chartres (later Bishop of London), and Graham Leonard the then bishop of London. Afterwards, before walking to the Fishmongers, a large group-photograph was taken of all two hundred and fifty participants, on the site of the block on Tower Green. Miles used to joke to journalists that, 'The Tower of London is to my family, what Wormwood Scrubs is to you lot.' All six successive heads of the Norfolk family in the late-fifteenth and sixteenth century had been attainted for treason, five of them being imprisoned in the Tower, three of them dying there, two of them beheaded, while the 1st Duke died in battle on Richard III's side at Bosworth in 1485.

In addition to celebrations in London and at Arundel, there were also events in Sheffield, where there is a large urban estate of the Norfolk family, and Norwich, the capital of the county of their title. We arranged an exhibition of works of art from Arundel and Carlton—paintings, tapestries, silver—which was displayed in Sheffield City Art Gallery where Julian Spalding was then director and which went on to the Castle Museum at Norwich in the autumn. The Lord Mayor (Mrs Hattersley) and Corporation of Sheffield put on an amazing banquet in the Victorian Town Hall for the occasion. I could not take my eyes off the mayoral chain of office draped over her ample front; it was a masterpiece of Edwardian silverwork by Omar Ramsden. Just as amazing was the feast itself: roast suckling pigs in aspic, caviar in ice constructions, and strawberries served in sugar swans. Those of us who were not socialists had never seen anything like it before.

I was appointed an Officer of Arms Extra Ordinary in 1982, as Fitzalan Pursuivant (in succession to Wilfrid Scott-Giles). I was later promoted to Maltravers Herald, taking part in ancient ceremonial, especially the State Opening of Parliament at Westminster and the Garter Service at Windsor every year. It is a royal appointment by Sign Manual, on the recommendation of the Earl Marshal. Trevor-Roper wrote an amused letter to Michael MacLagan (Fellow of Trinity, Oxford, and Richmond Herald). 'I see that my former protégé John Martin Robinson has become one of your College—I mean the College of Arms, not Trinity. A true piece of 18th century patronage. I sold him to Woodrow Wyatt to write a book on the Wyatt dynasty; from him he passed to Miles Norfolk as librarian (and has written in a fortnight a history of *that* dynasty for its 500th anniversary) ... I am glad to see that private patronage still exists.'

The Officers of Arms are members of the 'Ceremonial Royal Household'. Some years ago, the Queen gave an evening party at Buckingham Palace for ninety of the 'Ceremonials'. It was an unusual experience to mingle with the Keepers of the Royal Swans, Constables of Royal Castles, Clerks of the Closet, Gentlemen at Arms and the whole Gilbert and Sullivan cavalcade, amidst the Van Dycks, Rembrandts, Vermeers, Claudes, French ormolu, and rare black and gold chinoiserie Sèvres in George IV's Picture Gallery. My heraldic duties add a delightful Ruritanian dimension to life and are great fun. On Garter Day the heralds have a picnic lunch beforehand at Runnymede or at Cumberland Lodge in Windsor Great Park and a drinks party at the Deputy Ranger's Lodge for our guests from the Service, after the heralds, Household, and knights tea with strawberries and cream in St George's Hall, which is a perfect way to spend a sunny June day. In thirty-eight years as an Officer of Arms it has only rained once on Garter Day which is always Monday in Ascot week.

Picnic before the Garter Service at Windsor Castle, 1991. JMR with sister Felicity and nieces Hannah and Kate.

The Garter Service in St George's Chapel is a shortened, highly patriotic version of Evensong with favourite hymns and *two* verses of the National Anthem, trumpets, organ and choir. It is meticulously rehearsed the Friday before and so generally goes without a hitch. Even when there is one, it is difficult for the uninitiated to discern. The Bishop of Winchester is the Prelate and always reads the lesson. Once when King Juan Carlos of Spain was being installed, the Bishop went up to the lectern and found it empty; no bible there. With splendid sangfroid and without a blink, he announced in sonorous Anglican tones 'Let the Holy Scripture be brought forth'. If one had not seen from the corner of an eye an embarrassed canon scurrying into the vestry to retrieve the book, one would have assumed it was an extra solemnity only performed when a supernumerary royal knight was present at the service.

Well-rehearsed and solemn perfection is a feature of royal

ceremonial as it is performed in England and always has been. The Venetian Ambassador in the reign of Henry VII was impressed by the faultless seriousness and silence of Court ceremony in the Tudor royal palaces, so different from Italy with sweaty masters of ceremony running around, clicking their fingers.

When Bernard Norfolk went to Pope Paul VI's coronation in Rome in 1963, as official representative from Britain, he had a private audience afterwards in the Apostolic Palace of the Vatican. The Pope said, 'Earl Marshal, what do you think of our ceremonial', referring to by far the grandest ritual to have survived into the modern world, just then performed, complete with the *Sedia Gestatoria*, ostrich feather fans, the Noble Guard, the Tiara, Cardinal Deacons in mitres and dalmatics, silver trumpets and the Sistine Choir. The Duke replied, with a twinkle, 'I do not think, Your Holiness, that I can congratulate you on its organisation.' He was noted for his deadpan answers. When organising the Investiture of the Prince of Wales in the roofless ruin of Caernarvon Castle in 1967 he was asked by a thicko journalist what would happen if it rained? The response was 'We will get wet.'

When I was first involved with the heralds, Garter King of Arms, the 'head boy', was Sir Anthony Wagner, distinguished scholar and efficient man of business. He put the Heralds' finances on a sound footing for the future and his own writing was noted for meticulous scholarship. Some of his junior colleagues were rather jealous as he commuted from his house in Chelsea Square to the College in a Bentley which he parked in the forecourt. The combination of business acumen and scholarship is unusual, and certainly could not be applied to Wagner's successor, Colonel Colin Cole, an officer in the Territorials and habitué of El Vinos; he was stout, red-faced, irascible and not very competent. He made his dislike for me clear.

Cole's successor was Conrad Swan, much more intelligent and efficient, a Canadian who had served in the Indian army in the Second World War, then studied at Peterhouse. He had a romantic streak, and never got into a car if he could ascend into a horseless carriage. Sadly he had to retire early after he 'discovered' a document claiming his son-in-law had received a grant of arms a hundred years earlier than was the case, which enabled the latter to join the Order of Malta without expensive 'passage money'. Conrad was succeeded in 1995 by Peter Gwyn-Jones, step-brother of the travel writer Gavin Young.

Peter was a brilliant designer of new arms, drawing on his knowledge of ornithology and the natural world. His own crest was a coati, a type of American raccoon, which seemed appropriate. He died aged 70, and a carved and polychromed version of his coati crest (given him by colleagues) touchingly sat on the altar steps during his memorial service at St Martin-in-the-Fields. His successor and the current Garter, Thomas Woodcock, is an old friend, and northern neighbour. He, like 'one' was born at St Mary's, Mount Street, in Preston (although not a Catholic). I always joke that Bernard de Hoghton, I and Thomas must have been born (successively at two year intervals), in the same bed, as the place was so small.

Several other heraldic colleagues were friends including the recusant baronet, Henry Paston Bedingfeld of Oxburgh in Norfolk who was Norroy and Ulster King of Arms, and occasionally let me act as his 'Deputy Norroy' for the High Sheriff of Lancashire's Shield Hanging in Lancaster Castle. This takes place in the summer at the beginning of the Lancashire shrieval year, and is a picturesque ceremony with a service in the medieval priory church, the Judges and county officials in procession to and from the castle and an escort of mounted police with pikes and Victorian helmets. The shield hanging itself in the Georgian Gothick Shire Hall, followed by lunch amidst the classical pomp of the Edwardian Town Hall.

Henry used to tell a nice story about his grandfather, also Henry. At the Reformation, though Catholic, the Bedingfelds had retained their burial chapel in the medieval parish church at Oxburgh. One day in 1948 the butler gleefully announced at breakfast, 'Oh Sir Henry, the church spire collapsed in the night and has totally demolished the church. But *your* chapel has not been damaged at all'; reinforcing the view that God is a Catholic.

Another colleague-friend was Patric Dickinson, Richmond Herald (later Clarenceux King of Arms), who I knew through Robbie Lyle and Nicholas Banszky at Oxford and who was also a friend of Woodrow Wyatt. Woodrow noted once when we were listening to Petronella singing at the piano in Cavendish Avenue: Patric is 'sentimental and unmarried. John Robinson is not sentimental and also unmarried.' Patric had been President of the Union at Oxford, and Woodrow could not understand why he had chosen heraldry rather than politics for a career. To everyone else it seemed a no-brainer.

Patric was always social and a collector of people. He liked designing new arms for popular crooners rather than archbishops and Lord Mayors. He did arms for both Cliff Richard and Elton John. At his parties in the Earl Marshal's Court at the College of Arms, he used to gather together an assembly of literary, political, financial and eccentric lion cubs. He was best man at the banking fogey Michael Hodge's wedding in Balliol Chapel to Veronica Addington ('Pitt is to Addington as London is to Paddington'), known to her friends as 'Hon Vron'. The Hodges had announced their engagement at my house in Lancashire, one New Year when they were staying. It has been my experience that many friends have married other friends, which leaves me with a quandary as to where to sit in church: on the groom's side or on the bride's. Michael has always been a great church enthusiast and ecclesiologist. He often accompanied me on visits to freezing Marston Hall, in Lincolnshire, seat of the squarson and writer Henry Thorold.

Henry would drive us to remote places in the Wolds in his ancient Bentley with the windows wide open in February, himself inured to the East Winds blowing from Siberia, while declaiming on the architectural sights. I still see Lincolnshire through a Thorold lens and have adopted his archaic pronunciation of the places: 'Brant *Bruton*, Boothby *Paynel*, Grant-um'.

I met Henry at supper at Peter Howell's in Oxford, when he was chaplain at Summerfields. Most of his career had been spent at Lancing as House Master of Gibbs House, and where he taught

The Miller wedding in Staffordshire, 1986. The Best Man (JMR) and ushers in Brewood.

Latin, as Willie Gladstone put it, 'in the manner in which he imagined that he had been taught it.' (He had been a King's Scholar at Eton.) After Henry's death I organised two hatchments for him. One hung over the front door at Marston for a year and a day, the other was painted by boys in the art department at Lancing and hangs in the chapel there as a memorial.

I have been Best Man at a couple of weddings, and made it a point to keep the speeches short. I consider speeches at public events are an unwelcome Victorian innovation, to be curbed. At James Miller's wedding to Mary Gifford at Chillington in Staffordshire in 1986, we gave our speech in the central hall under John Soane's domed ceiling, very resonant. We had driven back from the service in Brewood church down the two mile oak avenue which is not usually used and had been opened up especially by Mary's father, Peter, and the verges mown for the occasion by the foresters. When David Wakefield, an arch fogey, married Caroline Ingilby later in the same year, the wedding was at Ripley Castle in Yorkshire, courtesy of her brother Thomas. Caroline's formidable widowed mother Diane, Lady Ingilby was not impressed by either the groom's or my speech. 'How extraordinary that those two clever boys are so hopeless at public speaking!'

In due course Caroline and David moved into Ogston Hall, Derbyshire, where the house and estate had been bought by David's father, a Nottinghamshire business man and was a little private world. It is a special place, a romantic, blackened Jacobethan pile with a tall clock tower, arranged around an inner courtyard, and approached by a long drive along the shore of a large lake, actually a beautiful naturalised reservoir. Henry Thorold in the Shell Guide to Derbyshire described it as a 'lakeside fairy castle'.

Over the years they have restored the house, converting the back parts into three or four flats, living in the main rooms which are 16th to 18th century in origin, though all remodelled by Hine of Nottingham. He was a Victorian 'rogue architect' whose most notable work was a similar Victorian re-vamping for the Hildyards of Flintham in Nottinghamshire (where I once discovered a fox in the ice house.) Ogston has been part of my annual weekend house peregrinations for forty years. Knowing a house over a long time allows you to watch change and improvement. At Ogston, one has the satisfaction of seeing the belt of native trees on the skyline across the Amber valley in front of the house, which I advised David to plant, grow into a proper 'Capability' landscape feature. I do not like bare skylines, and always encourage tree-planting to give a comforting sense of enclosure, and to differentiate between civilisation and the ordinary world outside.

A favourite country destination from 1978 was West Wratting Park in Cambridgeshire, about 6 miles from Newmarket. It is a beautiful red brick house with tall centre and flanking wings, and the main rooms with rococo ceilings. It had been built in the 18th century by Sir John Jacob, 3rd Bart, a racing man. After the war it was bought by Ursula and Erland d'Abo. In 1951 when they acquired it, the place was a derelict prep school and they had converted it back to a proper house, and built up an estate of a couple of thousand acres of good farm land. Ursula designed the garden and planted two *Magnolia Grandiflora* on the park front which are now as tall as the house itself, filling the rooms with their lemon scent when in flower. As she and Erland had a share in Mallets, the Bond Street antique dealers (where Martin Drury worked before joining the National Trust staff), they had been able to furnish it beautifully with good Georgian furniture.

Everything at West Wratting was done with great taste and style and there were huge arrangements of white sprayed foliage in glass containers as well as pot plants in season. Erland had died young, leaving Ursula a widow for fifty years; she lived to be over a hundred, dying in 2017. She reigned alone at West Wratting until her son Henry married and took over the estate. There she oversaw the garden and ran the house in a beautiful traditional manner which was an inspiration to me. There was a Portuguese butler and house-keeper, but she prepared much of the food herself. She was a good cook, a dab hand at a soufflé, having learnt as a child from her father's cook at Belvoir in the 1920s. When Henry took over she retired to London, first to her house in Kensington Square and then a flat looking over Ladbroke Square in Notting Hill.

I met Ursula and her huge frightening Doberman 'Mr Blue', when I was working on the Kensington volumes of the *Survey of London* for the GLC (organising measured drawings and photographs of the architecture). We became friends and she invited me regularly for the weekend to West Wratting. It was an easy train journey to the little station at Audley End. Once in the early days, the Edmund Vesteys came to lunch. I overheard them in the hall on arrival say 'Is this the young man you picked up in the Square in London?' I thought 'How rude', and then realised they were not talking about me, but the dog who had indeed adopted Ursula in the street and had never left her, loyal till death.

Ursula had an extraordinary life that spanned the 20th century. The oldest child of the 9th Duke of Rutland, she was born in

Ursula d'Abo and JMR, 1983. Ursula lived to be 100.

November 1916 not just into the purple but at the very pinnacle of the most civilised wing of the aristocracy, when Britain was still the greatest power in the world, dukes were rich and influential, and her relations among the cleverest and most beautiful people in the country. A child of the 'Souls', that band of Edwardian intellectual aesthetes, she was the niece of Diana Cooper, Marjorie Anglesey and Violet (Hetty) Elcho (widow of Hugo, one of the Immortals killed in the trenches in 1916). She was painted by Rex Whistler, photographed by Cecil Beaton, and written about by Chips Channon.

Her childhood was spent at the Rutland's two glorious seats, the medieval dream of Haddon Hall, in the Peak, and the Regency splendours of Belvoir Castle, and their Georgian town house in Arlington Street near to the Ritz, or with her grandmother Violet Rutland, a gifted artist and sculptor, at her stylish studio house in St John's Wood. Always her father's favourite, she had strong childhood memories of helping him restore Haddon, shinning up the scaffolding in the chapel to pick whitewash off the medieval murals, revealing St Christopher standing in swirly, fish-inhabited waters, or pouring molten lead onto the billiard table (stripped of baize) to make flat lead sheets. She always had a head for heights and would in later life climb up ladders herself to clean leaves from gutters or trim the *Magnolia Grandiflora* from the windows.

Ursula was a country woman. She ran the farm at West Wratting and we would walk down the lane on Saturday afternoons in winter to the dairy shed to see the cows being milked. When young she had ridden side-saddle and was a dashing figure in the Field. Her father disapproved of the 'fast set' around the Prince of Wales at Melton Mowbray and appointed an old groom to chaperone Ursula while out hunting, but she always left him behind as soon as they were out of sight. The Kennels of the Belvoir were just below the castle, and she loved visiting the hounds, the huntsmen and the kennel men. Another special friend on the estate was the pig man, and she was fascinated watching him prepare swill from wooden buckets of food leftovers. Belvoir was a large feudal family and she felt equally at home watching the cook in the kitchen, as dining with her father in full evening dress with a gardenia in his buttonhole, eating nectarines off Chelsea 'Dr Wall' plates.

Animals loved her and she had a St Francis-like gift of being able to tame them. At different times she made companions of unpromisingly daunting fauna. A fierce parrot with a huge razor-like beak able, as Ursula gleefully noted, to slice off a finger with a snip, used to sit on her shoulder gently nuzzling her ear and 'Mr Blue', the huge killer Doberman never left her side, drooling in docile adoration, while everyone else gave him a very wide berth

Her family were at lunch in the Great Hall at Haddon in September 1939 when the Duke announced dramatically, 'we shall never sit here again like this, we are at war with Germany'. She had a narrow escape in the London blitz when the house where she was sleeping received a direct hit and she was rescued through a first floor window from the tottering ruin. She returned to Belvoir where her father had become an honorary keeper of the Public Record Office and was looking after the National Archives which had been evacuated there from Chancery Lane for safety. Ursula paused just long enough in London to rescue the family jewels from Drummonds Bank and take them to the shelter of the castle, too. As for so many of her generation, the war was a liberation and an enlargement of horizons. She worked for the duration at a munitions factory in Grantham, supervising 2000 women making shells. She commuted from Belvoir by moonlight in a pony trap, often so tired that she fell asleep and the pony found its own way home along the avenue from Redmile.

In 1943 she married Anthony Marreco, then an officer in the Fleet Air Arm, but a brilliant young barrister, a prosecutor at Nuremberg, and a Human Rights campaigner, who was a co-founder with Peter Benenson of Amnesty International. They divorced in 1947. Tired and depressed, she accepted an invitation from 'Jai', the glamorous Maharajah of Jaipur to go to India for a year, for some sun and food. She flew in a flimsy military aeroplane from London over the Arabian deserts, touching down amidst wild tribesmen like a Lady Hester Stanhope from the skies. She saw India under the last refulgent rays of the Raj, and Jaipur in all its princely glory, pink palaces, garlands of jasmine, elephants, peacocks, jewels; the lot. She also met the Indian Nationalists and made a great friend of Nehru who corresponded with her for years. Back in England, she married Erland d'Abo, a banker, in 1951. After Erland's death she became close to Paul Getty, acting as his hostess at Sutton Place. On his death she was one of the 'girl-friends' (as the Press called them) who received generous bequests, including a Matisse drawing which she hung in the lavatory at West Wratting.

Another house which has been a destination now for over 40 years is Dalmeny in Scotland. Dalmeny and its predecessor Barnbougle Castle, restored as a library retreat by the Prime Minister 5th Earl of Rosebery, enjoy a sublime site in a large Georgian park on the south shore of the Firth of Forth between Edinburgh and South Queensferry. The place commands vast views eastward over the grey waters towards the North Sea. Big ships, oil and gas tankers and naval frigates coming to Rosyth for maintenance, traverse the waves. In the middle distance are the shores of Fife, rocky islands, Leith with its white silhouetted modern developments gleaming like a fortified Kasbah, Arthur's Seat, Edinburgh Castle and the Pentland Hills, and in the far distance the volcanic outline of North Berwick Law. Beyond the park to the west, seen on walks to the wooded promontory of Hound's Point haunted by the medieval Sir Roger Moubray's loyal Crusader dog, are the Forth Bridges, heroic masterpieces of British engineering, especially the red-lead painted steel Railway Bridge.

The whole place with its views and large-scale landscape feels like the capital of a maritime empire, which of course it was when the 5th Earl of Rosebery was three times Foreign Secretary, Lord President of the Council, Liberal Leader in the House of Lords, and Prime Minister in succession to Gladstone whose famous Midlothian Campaign he masterminded. One could imagine the Victorian Grand Fleet steaming up the Forth.

I often went to Dalmeny for the Edinburgh Festival in August and for New Year when there were exhausting Scottish reels in the Staircase Hall. We would also go over to Murthly in Perthshire at New Year, home of Robert Steuart Fothringham (one of the three Fothringham boys at Fort Augustus). There we played 20-a-side football in the avenue in front of the castle with Robert acting as the referee, tooting on the hunting horn. Even in my 30s that was too strenuous, and we left it to the prep school generation to do all the real running around.

In the early days, Dalmeny was being repaired, dry rot eradicated, and the contents rearranged to include the things saved from Mentmore in Buckinghamshire when that house was sold following the death of Neil Rosebery's father. The family live upstairs at Dalmeny with a new kitchen installed by Professor Dunbar-Nasmith of the Edinburgh School of Architecture. There are wonderful views from up there. Downstairs is open to the public and the big rooms are displayed as a museum for the astonishing Rosebery collection of French furniture, tapestries and

Sèvres, Napoleonic relics, and dazzling historic portraits, though the dining room and library are used.

I wrote two articles for *Country Life* showing the restored rooms. Once for a large dinner party, James Miller who was also staying and I got out masses of silver, a wine cooler the size of a bath, the 5th Earl's Racing Trophies (he won the Derby with Ladas) and huge candelabra, and spent all day cleaning them. One of the dour Modernist Scottish guests commented disapprovingly of the glittering table that he thought it looked 'decadent'.

Even more interesting than Dalmeny was Barnbougle, on the shore of the Firth of Forth, half a mile from its 1814 Regency Tudor replacement designed by William Wilkins. Reduced to a ruin, the old castle had been restored in 1881 by the Prime Minister, 5th Earl of Rosebery, as a scholar's retreat for his Scottish books. There he could read, write and practise his speeches. It had 6 libraries, housing 10,000 books, but only one bedroom with a simple iron bedstead for him, and one bathroom with a marble bath fed with salt water pumped from the Forth. On his death in 1926 the castle had been closed up, and survived unchanged. A housekeeper lived on the ground floor and dusted all the books every year.

When one first knew it, the place was an atmospheric private shrine. The Prime Minister's red dispatch boxes were still on his desk, and his washing china still on his bedroom dressing table. It was an astonishing place redolent of historical romance. The rooms were full of family portraits and personal and antiquarian collections. We used to go over and browse. Now it has all been beautifully restored and opened to the public and let for events. The fin-de-siècle decoration and light fittings all survive but obviously the forlorn and sad romance still lingering in the 1980s has been superseded by new life.

I got involved with the Roseberys and Dalmeny as a result of Mentmore, the Rothschild house in the Vale of Aylesbury, inherited from Hannah Rothschild, wife of the Prime Minister. As a schoolboy, the 5th Earl said he would marry an heiress, win the Derby and become Prime Minister. He achieved all three. The

Rosebery trustees had generously offered Mentmore and its collection in lieu of death duties in 1976 for the modest sum of £3 million, but the twilight Labour Government mishandled the negotiations and turned the arrangement down. The spectacular ensemble was broken up in a huge Sotheby's sale; the Roseberys themselves selecting key items and transferring them to Scotland, as a continuing Rothschild element of the family collections, now concentrated in the northern houses at Dalmeny, Barnbougle and Rosebery.

A group of us embarked on a heroic campaign to save Mentmore in 1976/7. It was one of SAVE's first fully-fledged public fights outside Spitalfields. When the government turned down Neil Rosebery's offer of the house and collections, nobody knew what the house contained, as it had always been intensely private. We decided to publish an illustrated pamphlet showing what was at stake, the splendour of the architecture and the marvellous treasures within. *'Save Mentmore for the Nation, A great house and collection for the first time in print'*, was the pioneer of SAVE's many campaigning publications. It sold for 40p a copy including postage.

The accompanying press release threw down the gauntlet: 'In refusing to acquire Mentmore Towers, Buckinghamshire, and its fabulous collections the Government has missed one of the greatest art-bargains in history.' The pamphlet was put together by Marcus, and John Harris, curator of the RIBA Drawings Collection (in whose office our campaign meetings took place), William Allen then the editor of *Connoisseur*, me and Simon Jervais of the Furniture and Woodwork Department at the V&A, described anonymously as 'an expert'. We got our information and the illustrations from the rare privately printed catalogue of her father's collection by Hannah de Rothschild (1890) of which there was a copy in the National Art Library at the V&A, to which 'an expert' had easy access.

The SAVE pamphlet sparked off a debate in the National Press, in which we enlisted the support of various MPs including Patrick

SAVE

MENTMORE FOR THE NATION

The SAVE pamphlet for Mentmore, the pioneer of SAVE's many campaigning publications.

Cormack who has always been a 'heritage' champion. He asked an 'emergency question' in the Commons and wrote the 'Inside story of the Mentmore "disaster"' in the *Sunday Telegraph*, which he attributed to 'official dithering and lack of vision'. There was a debate in the House of Lords where Marcus, Simon and I sat in the peeress's gallery to watch the proceedings.

The government minister responsible was the Under Secretary at the Department of the Environment, Baroness Birk. She made a striking figure among the subfusc hereditary peers who packed the Chamber. She was wearing a sort of cat suit of orange suede which matched the orange tint of her hair. Sadly, her flat-footed answers did not match the dazzle of her wardrobe. She was unable to answer questions as to why the Land Fund, set up by the Labour Chancellor Hugh Dalton in 1946 as a war memorial with £50 million from the sale of surplus army equipment, could not provide the £3 million required.

The Land Fund was specifically dedicated to the acquisition of British historic buildings and 'landscapes of outstanding natural beauty' as a thanksgiving for Victory over the Nazis. Alas, the fund was not ring-fenced and had been raided by Macmillan's government, one of the most philistine in English history, responsible for the destruction of the Euston Arch, the Coal Exchange, the Cornmarket in Oxford and the wrecking of the West End skyline with monstrosities like the Hilton Hotel. A few million may still have been in the kitty in 1977, but the Treasury was unyielding: they claimed there was no money.

We lost the Mentmore battle, but we won the War. The Heritage Lottery Fund was set up as an independent body, as a direct result, and has helped purchase numerous buildings, landscapes and works of art over the last 40 years. In the event, the Government spent more on buying a handful of major works of art for the National Museums than they could have acquired the whole place for intact. The lots broke all records, including two coal scuttles which fetched £900. Peter Simple of the *Daily Telegraph*, poked fun at the inflated prices in his 'Way of the World' column, 'Objects purporting to come from Mentmore are turning up all over the country. Yesterday Mrs Linda Gropes, a typical housewife of Torres Vedras Road, Nerdley, was proudly displaying a pair of eight foot high gilded plastic garden gnomes, both sitting on gilded mushrooms ... "They make me feel I have a sort of rapport, however small, with England's stately heritage of civilization."' The *Daily Mail* was more concerned with what it saw as a Common Market 'rip-off' with French and German art dealers hoovering up the treasures.

As for poor Mentmore itself, that beautiful Victorian prodigy house by Joseph Paxton and his son-in-law, Stokes, based on Wollaton Hall and built of golden Ancaster Stone in 1852, the interior lined with 18th century French boiseries, cut velvet hangings from Stowe, and a chimney-piece from Rubens House in Antwerp, languishes empty and decaying. For a time it belonged to a Maharishi sect who levitated in the empty rooms, but after them it has passed through a series of bankrupt hotel developers. It could still be 'saved'. The ideal would be for a Rothschild led Trust to buy it from the Receiver and to transfer there some of the collections from other Rothschild houses and to open it in conjunction with Waddesdon, maroon liveried buses emblazoned with the five arrows, shuttling back and forth between them.

Mentmore was sold, and the empty house languished forlorn, but Arundel was saved and provided a preservation model for all the most important houses in England and Scotland. When Bernard Norfolk died in 1975, he bequeathed the castle to the National Trust, or if not accepted, to an independent family-run trust such as had first been considered in the 1950s, but was not then possible. Miles did not want the castle to go to the National Trust and preferred the other option. Fortunately, the National Trust wanted an endowment of over a million pounds which the family Trustees could not provide as the estates were all in discretionary trusts for specified beneficiaries, and the art collection and contents of the castle were entailed on Miles, so the Trust was unable to accept it.

During the War Miles had served in Italy with Colonel Healey, later the Labour Chancellor of the Exchequer. Miles now went to see Denis Healey at the Treasury and explained his problem. Healey told him there was a new Bill going through Parliament which might make a dedicated historic buildings trust possible, and advised him to talk with the Leader of the House of Lords. He did, and it was possible. Arundel was vested in a charitable trust in 1976 with an endowment from the renewal of the leases of the Strand Estate in London. Since then the fabric has been repaired, the interior restored to Victorian splendour, new gardens laid out, the collections augmented, and the public opening run as a successful business which makes an annual profit.

It is an instructive contrast to what might have happened had Arundel gone to the National Trust. The castle would have been preserved in its post-War doldrums, devoid of major treasures, the family rooms empty, the walled garden a car park, and the place would not have been lived in again. No doubt well-maintained by bureaucracy, it would have lacked the flair, imagination, sense of purpose and additional funding that the family have been able to give it. The castle continues to be run as a fully staffed, meticulously maintained great house which serves as the focus of the local economy and community, the capital of a great estate, as well as being a well-loved show place for visitors with the highest rating on Trip Advisor of any English country house open to the public. It has been available to tourists since the 18th century.

When Miles's eldest son, Edward married Georgina Gore in 1987 they made the joint decision to move back into the castle which had not been lived in since 1959 when Bernard and his wife Lavinia had moved with some of the best furniture and pictures, to a new neo-Georgian house in the park designed by Claud Phillimore and which served as Lavinia Norfolk's dower house until her death in 1995. Eddie and Georgie have redecorated, rearranged and revived the whole of the castle, starting with the library where the worn out 1846 carpet has been rewoven to the original pattern, and all the Morant cut velvet upholstered seat furniture (banished to the attic after the War) reinstated on the evidence of

Victorian photographs and water colours, with the advice of the late Clive Wainwright, a bearded William Morris look-alike from the V&A 'woodworm' department.

The library was followed by the family rooms in the east wing which Georgie re-furnished and decorated with the help of David Mlinaric, a genius; then the state rooms open to the public; then the guest bedrooms upstairs with ample four-posters replacing meagre post-war divans, and numerous new bathrooms. It is now all very comfortable, while traditions like log fires in the main bedrooms (and bathrooms) for winter house parties are maintained. In the 1970s, there were fewer bathrooms, the decoration had not been touched since the 1930s and 40s, and the house was not very warm. Anne Norfolk dubbed it Colditz, while someone-else described the ground floor with its empty whitewashed gothic revival passages as looking like a bankrupt convent. It doesn't now.

The stonework has been cleaned. The walls bristle with antlers and armour, old oak furniture and mahogany framed glass cases of stuffed birds populate and furnish the once empty vistas. It all looks authentically untouched Victorian, but all of it has been revived and reconstituted since the 1980s.The main rooms were always splendid, having been reopened to the public in 1947 after army occupation, but are now even more magnificent with returned Canalettos, Reynoldses, Norfolk House furniture, porcelain, silver and gold plate from Park House. The library is used for tea after shoots, the big dining room when there are more than 20 for weekend house parties, the billiard room for post-prandial games of Freda, the Barons Hall for the estate Christmas Party with a giant Christmas tree and log fires in both the huge Violet-le-Duc inspired chimney-pieces.

Arundel is of course a Catholic house with a magnificent vaulted Gothic private chapel, a late-14th century burial chapel, the Fitzalan Chapel (originally a collegiate foundation), attached to the parish church, and a vast Gothic church in the town built by the 15th Duke to mark his coming of age in 1868, which now serves as the Catholic Cathedral for the diocese of Arundel and

Brighton. Since the 19th century, life has part-revolved round the Catholic liturgical year. Memorial masses are said in the Fitzalan Chapel on All Souls Day in November, and the anniversary days of the dukes buried there. The castle chapel is dedicated to Our Lady, and the feast of the Immaculate Conception in December is treated as the patronal feast with a choral mass open to the public. Afterwards there are drinks in the Barons Hall. Warming myself in front of the fire one year, I encountered an unknown woman and introduced myself. 'Oh, I am the priest's wife,' she said. Her husband, the parish priest at Petworth, was a re-ordained Anglican convert, and though Catholic priests of course are celibate, some of the recent ex-Anglicans were already married.

The high point of the Catholic year at Arundel is the feast of Corpus Christi in June. After High Mass in the Cathedral, there is a procession of the Blessed Sacrament accompanied by the picturesque papal knights—the Knights of Malta, the Knights of the Holy Sepulchre and the Knights of St Gregory, through the town to the castle and benediction in the quadrangle at an altar framed by palm trees and flowering shrubs in pots which takes the gardeners three days to arrange. On the first occasion I took part in 1976, I noted with satisfaction that the Lodge Keeper at the High Street Gate doffed his top hat twice, first to the Blessed Sacrament, carried by the Bishop under its canopy flanked by acolytes, then to the Duke walking immediately behind as the procession entered the grounds, preceded by the First Communicants strewing flower petals and followed by a large congregation. The Corpus Christi procession at Arundel was instituted by the 15th Duke in 1870, on the pattern of those he had seen in Italy. A special feature is the carpet of flowers down the nave of the cathedral, the flowers laid in mosaic-like patterns by the parishioners and reminiscent of the flower carpets of Sicily. It is wonderful that this colourful and pious celebration has survived and still flourishes amidst the appropriate Gothic Revival townscape of Arundel and its castle and Cathedral.

The Kazan Cathedral, St Petersburg, 1981. Glynn Boyd Harte, Simon Rendall, JMR, James Miller in phalanx framed by giant Corinthian columns. (Gavin Stamp).

5
Abroad

ABROAD OR 'Foreign Parts', for me means Italy, Germany, France, Spain, and Portugal, and only occasional visits out of Europe. I do not indulge in Real Travel. I have never been to Africa (despite half my family living in Cape Town), Australia, China and Japan, or the deserts of Arabia, or the Arctic and Antarctic, nor wanted to. I am not a Thesinger or a Chatwin, though a member of the Travellers Club for over forty-five years. The travel qualification for that, however, is only 500 miles in a straight line, on land, from London. The last part of the condition was added when a founder-member pointed out: 'otherwise convicts in Botany Bay would have been eligible'. I am hefted to western civilisation just as my local Herdwick sheep only graze the fells where the Vikings placed them over a thousand years ago. But I have been to America and Russia which can claim to be additions to western civilization.

I first visited the United States in 1976, bicentennial year, the 200th anniversary of the adoption of the Declaration of Independence by the colonists. My initial memory of New York, coming in from J.F.K. airport through the dreary south-eastern suburbs of Queens, was of the Manhattan skyline in the distance with the Empire State Building floodlit in red, white and blue stripes. The patriotic theme was continued the following morning when, going for a walk in Central Park, I encountered a woman with a white poodle which had been clipped and dyed to represent the stars and stripes. That was just the beginning. All the buses, fire hydrants and street benches were painted in red, white and blue stripes. That first impression still seems to me to be an accurate thumbnail of America, its wackiness and sense of patriotism, the contrast between the Hi-Rise 'Biggest Economy in the World', glitzy temples of corporate capitalism, and the sprawling, infinite-seeming suburbs which were not obviously prosperous.

In the 1970s, places like Queens made Hounslow and Ealing seem smart by comparison, the latter still with well-kept 1930s Metroland architecture and neat privet-hedged gardens. Now, of course, the pre-war suburbs of London are teeming slums, packed with the poor of the world. You are offered drugs on the streets at 10 o'clock in the morning in places like Willesden. The houses have been stripped of proper painted joinery and real Crittall windows (manufactured by Lord Braintree), which have all been replaced with flammable, cancer-inducing, toxic UPVC, the brickwork disfigured with cheap cement render, ugly pebble-dash and ubiquitous satellite dishes (to watch 'sport' and pornography). The former front gardens have been concreted over, the green hedges or picket fences ripped out, to make parking spaces for broken junk and dirty jalopies. The greatest sociological and architectural difference between the London I knew in the 1960s and 1970s and now, has been the deterioration of the rings of twentieth century outer suburbs, while the 'inner city'—places like Notting Hill and Islington which had been slums—is now 'gentrified', renovated and smart. Not that even forty or fifty years ago, one ever came across anyone who lived in the hundreds of thousands of houses in the 1930s belt. It was a joke when driving out on the A4 or the A1 past miles of identical half-timbered pre-war 'semis': 'Do you know who owns these or who lives over there?' 'Only Thomas Lyttelton' was the answer, or with a wave towards Winchmore Hill, 'And, of course, Roy Strong was born over there.'

(After I had written this, I was looking through some old papers of my great uncle William's Settlement and discovered that my family had owned the ground rents of twenty houses in Drayton Road, West Ealing W13, until sold in 1942. I knew about our more extensive ground rents in Handsworth, Edgbaston, Smethwick, Kings Norton and six other parishes in Birmingham, sold at the same time, but I hadn't realised that we also had some London ground rents. So I could have replied from the back of the car ... 'and me' to the 'who owns these?')

The contrast with the first impression of New York for a Londoner is not as clear-cut now as it was then. Another surprise for a first visitor was American class differences. Just as I had naively imagined that the United States were universally rich, so I had swallowed the line that they were classless. I got a shock looking at paintings in the Met, when I tried to address an elderly warder about a picture hanging behind him and was met by Bateman cartoon astonishment and uncomprehending silence; nobody had ever deigned to speak to him before. In the National Gallery in London, it has always seemed natural to comment on a Titian or Rubens to the member of staff sitting beside it, like talking to a farmer about his sheep or grass; after all, the warders look at the pictures all day, and I have found they often have something interesting to say. The same 'distance' is true of the staff in American houses, hotels and clubs where there is none of the friendly, 'feudal familiarity' of Britain; even many of the taxi drivers seem cut-off, unless they are recent immigrants from India, in which case they are more on the wave-length of a Briton and are relieved to be able to chat comfortably with a passenger.

My hosts on early visits to New York were a mixture of impecunious contemporaries, graduate students and juniors in the art-trade on the one hand, or on the other, older, richer Americans met while acting as a cicerone for cultural tours in England. They had the names of new wings in art museums or buildings on Ivy League campuses. They asked me to come and stay in Greenwich, Connecticut, Back Bay, Boston, or near the Baltimore Country Club, so I did. They were hospitable and charming, and had the natural good manners that is such an attractive characteristic of educated East Coasters. They treated people as if they were more important than was the case, which was very endearing.

Their houses, though small by English standards, were attractive but difficult to date. Were they genuine eighteenth or nineteenth century or 1936 Colonial Revival? The gardens, even when they stretched to acres were disconcertingly called 'yards'. They often owned 'nice things'. Mr Saks, (grandson of Horace Saks of the store on Fifth Avenue) lived in Connecticut in a house which he had designed himself in French *dixhuitième* style. It had an oval staircase winding round a Clodian-type group of marble cupids; the hall was hung with French Old Master drawings by Callot and contemporaries; the drawing room was panelled with Louis XV boiserie, while the dining room had a Napoleonic *papier peint*, and Thomire silver gilt epergnes on the side tables. The library was the heart of the house, for he was a serious bibliophile and trustee of the Morgan Library. His speciality was Venetian books from the fourteenth to the eighteenth century, and he also had a Kelmscott Chaucer. He not only collected rare books, but was very hands on in their care and maintenance, with a workshop where he did his own bindings to a professional standard, with all the fine leather and tools needed for stamped gilt decoration. I wish now I had asked him how he had trained.

Student-bohemian friends lived in less luxury, mainly in dilapidated apartments in crumbly brownstones on the west side, infested with cockroaches which breed and spread in New York's communal steam-heating system. You had to be careful if you got up in the middle of the night not to crunch them under bare feet. Astonishingly, in such places the bathroom opened straight off the kitchen with no lobby such as required by English health and building regulations. It is more difficult going for a pee in a London flat or office and having to negotiate multiple self-closing doors, than emerging out of a submarine escape hatch.

The seeming complete disregard in America for 'Health and Safety' and all the petty childish regulations that bedevil every aspect of English life is very striking. Years later, when writing a short history of Asprey's for the then owners of the firm (a Japanese-Canadian consortium), I visited their short-lived New York outlet in the Trump Tower on Fifth Avenue, while it was being remodelled by the London designer David Mlinaric. It was astonishing to see the helmet-less builders in T-shirts and gym shoes dodging around nail-studded joinery. In London they would have had to wear metal-plated boots, asbestos proof gloves, hard hats and hi-viz, day-glo tabards. (New York builders, by the way, have better health and live longer than their cosseted English counterparts.)

Joseph (Joe) Miller, a graduate student met in Oxford, lived with a Canadian friend Gordon, a lecturer in English literature at Princeton; they had an apartment up near Columbia. Getting there was an exciting journey on the subway for the uninitiated; if you caught the train on the wrong level you were whisked past, to the northern tip of Manhattan and the Cloisters, that improbable Rockefeller-funded assemblage of Italian and Spanish medieval fragments. Joe, who came from Ohio, had a splendid sardonic humour and a startling way of putting things. He took me to Brecht's *Threepenny Opera* at the Lincoln Centre (he was serious about culture) and described the audience walking up the red-carpetted, red-walled stairs of the opera house as 'just like corpuscles flowing up veins'. He would not let me admire the white marble, soft-modern symmetries of the Lincoln Centre. He loathed the huge crystal chandeliers and thought it all the acme of vulgarity, full of people in 'double knit leezure suits', except the doormen in gold braid. It is just a 'temple of kitsch', he replied to my faint attempted compliments. Talking about men in uniforms, he said, 'It is politically retrograde to lust after policemen. That's why I do it.' His was the sort of American humour summed up in a cartoon in the New Yorker in 1977: Moses and the Israelites on the banks of the Red Sea like a scene by John Martin. God in glory, rolling back the waters with flashes of thunder and lightning to reveal a path through. The Israelites to Moses, 'You don't expect us to walk through all that mud, do you?'

While Joe and I went to the opera and art museums, and discussed Elizabethan recusant literature, Gordon had other things on his mind in the evenings. When he got back from Princeton, he used to dress up in his uniform of lumberjack plaid shirt and Levis, and disappear downtown to the Village, not to be seen again until the next day. The mid-1970s was the heyday of Gay New York, enjoying the freedom that followed the Stonewall Riots of 1969 and before Aids struck. Joe and Gordon insisted I must go to one of the clubs in Greenwich Village after supper one evening: 'an essential sight for any visitor to New York'. They thought the Mine Shaft in the Meat Packing District might be a bit too much for a sheltered Englishman, so took me to the Anvil which had been founded in 1974. It was a bit different from Annabels in Berkeley Square, especially the dress code and prices. Entrance was $3 and you got two drinks for that. It comprised a ground floor reception and small basement rooms. It was dark, with grey painted walls, sawdust sprinkled floors and naked black boys dancing on the bar top. The constricted space was packed with identikit stocky cowboys sporting identical moustaches. They had pseudo-aggressive, hustler manners which rather contrasted with their gentle, mid-western voices if they spoke. One suspects many were country boys, escaped to the Big City. The end, of course, was tragic, for the downtown clubs which were all closed as a health risk in the 1980s, were the main spreader of the Aids epidemic, and many of the young habitués died a couple of years after my visit, including Joe's friend, tragic, handsome, clever, Canadian Gordon. And those Englishmen I knew who died of Aids, contracted it from visits to New York, like Jeffery Daniels, director of the Geoffrye Museum in Shoreditch, Gervase Jackson-Stops, my colleague at *Country Life*, and John Bristol who I started to help write his memoirs but they never got further than an article in the *Sunday Express*. They depended on his then current notoriety and matey stories about Warhol, and nobody was interested after he was dead.

Not everybody in New York inhabited cockroach-infested slums, though much of the fabric of Manhattan remains surprisingly Victorian, like a pre-First World War version of Liverpool or Glasgow. Some friends had more modern apartments on the Upper East Side. Those working in the sale rooms, for instance, often had attractive accommodation provided by their employers at Sotheby's or Christie's. Colin Sheaf, who had been a contemporary aficionado of Fr James's porcelain seminars at the Ashmolean, had after Oxford joined Christie's, and was their oriental porcelain man in New York in the mid-1970s. (He is now global head of Asian Art for the Bonhams Group.) When I first visited New York, he had a pleasant Christie's apartment near the Metropolitan Museum.

Brenda Auslander, who worked for Sotheby's, was kindness itself and not only let me stay at her apartment, but organised little dinner parties to introduce the arts *monde*. She seemed to me an archetypal New York girl with a loud voice, abrasive humour, and a taste for strongly coloured clothes, especially purple. Purple was so associated with Brenda, that we gave her name to a particular shade. When travelling around for years after, and seeing a purple car or a painted house, we would comment, 'Oh look—a Brenda front door.' She had all sorts of mannerisms of speech which struck me as typically American, but may just have been Brenda's own idiosyncrasies. For instance, when helping her clear after her supper parties, I would be given the job of washing the silver knives and forks which she always referred to as her 'sterling'—'can you dry the Sterling please'. I would have thought this pretentious if I had not been in America.

Friends working for Sotheby's or Christie's provided a useful general network of berths for the impecunious traveller in the 1970s and 1980s, and not just in the States but in Europe too. Johnnie Mennel who I met at Civitella Ranieri in Umbria in 1969, had gone on to become Sotheby's representative in Rome where he had a palatial flat. Sotheby's also maintained a big apartment in Madrid, conveniently adjacent to the Prado and sometime later James Miller, Deirdre Rosebery and I spent a week there while admiring Velasquez and El Greco. The only disturbing thing about it was that unbeknown to us Spanish parking rules changed in the middle of the night and the permitted zone moved from one side of the street to the other. The first morning in Madrid we were horrified to find that the hired car had disappeared, we assumed stolen. Then we noticed that it had mysteriously flown across the road in the night. We wondered how. Did the Spanish traffic police have a master key for all vehicles or had they lifted it physically? We took the hint and thereafter conscientiously moved the car from side to side in the street at the prescribed times in the evening.

In 1976 and subsequent visits to the U.S., I rarely stayed in a hotel, but relied on the generosity of friends or, after election to the Travellers in London in 1978, exploited the 'reciprocals' with American clubs in New York, Boston and Washington. Most Englishmen are hugely in awe and appreciative of American hospitality. When we English say, 'You must come and stay', it is just a turn of phrase and we would be hugely put out if somebody landed on the doorstep with a large suitcase. The Americans, however, genuinely mean it. People I hardly knew in New York, friends of friends who might once have worked for Ben Weinreb, the architectural book dealer, and that sort of vague connection, arranged special dinner parties with carefully chosen guests to provide architectural or scholarly contacts.

I was and remain hugely grateful, and not a little guilty. With a mixture of naivety and selfishness, their hospitality was taken for granted. It is amazing that the charming upper class Americans such as those I had bear-led round English and Scottish country houses on a Connoisseur-National Trust tour in 1973 should have remained kind, personal friends and insisted one visited and stayed with them in the States. Some of them I kept up with for years, exchanging letters and Christmas cards. The Andersons in their Maryland Colonial-era house, Powder Mill Spring, outside Baltimore, were especially kind to me. Their house was delightful with lots of books, Georgian green-painted rooms, portraits on the walls, hats on the hall table, and 'American Chippendale' furniture. (Much 'American' Georgian furniture is, of course Irish and was bought up by New York dealers during the Irish Civil War and its destructive aftermath in the 1920s.)

He had been a colonel in the army and had fought in the Second World War, and looked rather like Ike. He was charmingly conservative (small c), wearing suits and spending his days at the

Ruxton Country Club. Anna was more intellectual and came from an academic family. Her father had been dean of Harvard and her sister was married to a professor there. Anna Anderson gave me an introduction to her sister in a house in Cambridge, Massachusetts when I went to Boston. This sort of kind help, was normal. Anna herself wrote books. I still have a novel she gave me, *The Woman in a Wrap Around Skirt*.

They took time off and drove me all over the place to visit historic buildings; into downtown Baltimore to see Benjamin Latrobe's Catholic cathedral (influenced in its design by James Wyatt of whom, however, Latrobe had a low opinion, dismissing him as being in the second rank of architects). We also visited the campus of Johns Hopkins University and the Walters Art Gallery of which Anna was a trustee and introduced me to the curator Dorothy Hill, and she took me to lunch in the Mount Vernon Club, of which the most famous member was Wallis Simpson. Anna also introduced me to her friend Betty Lee, born Cromwell, who despite her maiden name was an old American Catholic going back to the foundation of Maryland as a recusant colony. Betty turned out to know Trafford Klots, the American artist who lived in France and painted the portrait of Miles as a young man in his Grenadiers uniform which hangs in the Bow Drawing Room at Carlton.

The Andersons took me to dinner in delightful restaurants in and around Baltimore, like the Chesapeake Bay, specialising in sea food, or Hirondelle at the Ruxton Country Club. They showed me all the Georgian houses in the vicinity which they thought would interest me, such as the Carroll House in Baltimore itself and the Hampton House outside, which is the largest eighteenth century house in America, and they took me to Annapolis in Anne Arundel County (not pronounced as we pronounce Arundel, and in fact called after the Arundells of Wardour in Wiltshire, not the castle in Sussex).

Annapolis is one of the best small historic towns in America, a seventeenth and eighteenth century planned layout like Whitehaven or Maryport which it echoed on the other side of the Atlantic. It had good old buildings: the Capital of Maryland, St John's College (founded in 1696), St Anne's Church, and the picturesque City Dock, and of course the naval academy with its large domed classical chapel containing the crypt mausoleum of the revolutionary sailor John Paul Jones from Whitehaven, whom some English regard as a traitor-pirate (but I kept that thought to myself). The academy was wondrously traditional; the juniors being called 'plebes' before graduating to midshipmen, which reminded me of the 'bejants' at St Andrews.

Of particular interest were the late Colonial Era mansions in the town, notably the Chase-Lloyd House, the Hammond-Harwood House built in 1774, inspired by Palladio's Villa Pisani (according to the guidebook, but quite a long way after) and the Paca House of William Paca, a signatory of the Declaration of Independence exactly 200 years earlier. The terraced garden there was being authentically restored to the original design in 1976, having been rescued from degradation as the bus station car park for ADOT (The Annapolis Department of Transportation).

The American approach to conservation of historic areas and buildings was impressive. Restoration work was very active in the aftermath of international Conservation Year in 1975. Much was being done by rich individuals, private charities and local societies. In England there was, of course, the National Trust which in the 1970s was at the height of its influence as a national preservation charity, leading in the restoration, preservation, display and curatorship of historic buildings and landscapes. I served on the regional National Trust committee in the Lake District for ten years, at a time when it was pioneering the revival of lime mortar and traditional colour washes for vernacular buildings, and was changing attitudes from regarding the landscape as grass and trees to an understanding of it as a work of art, a Picturesque, designed Georgian and Victorian landskip. The National Trust's most famous beauty spot in the Lakes, Tarn Howes, for instance, was an artificial piece of water made and planted in the eighteenth and nineteenth centuries by the Marshall family from Leeds.

In America, one was struck by the dynamism of local non-profit organisations like the Maryland Historical Society, founded in 1844 and based in the Enoch Pratt House in Baltimore. Such charities depended on generous benefactors. This was especially the case with the Preservation Society of Newport which I encountered when I went to stay with Christopher Monkhouse at Rhode Island when he was working as a curator at Brown University there. He ended his career as director of European Decorative Arts at the Art Institute of Chicago and, now retired, he lives in his own well-preserved 19th century house in upstate New York, but in those early days he occupied a white clapboard house at Providence. He took me to see the Gilded Age *beaux arts* 'summer houses' at Newport, dubbed by Joe Crook the 'Gross Trianons'. Many of these were owned and curated by the Newport Preservation Society which had been founded by Katherine and Jeremy Warren in 1945, and endowed by the Vanderbilts. It was a model of such an American society.

Looking at American historic buildings, and practical preservation was as much a reason for going to the USA in 1976 as the kind invitations of the 'Connoisseurs' as I still think of them, and my book researches looking at architectural drawings in the Print Room of the Metropolitan and Cooper Hewitt museums in New York, and visiting my co-Wyatt enthusiast Fran Fergusson in Massachusetts. She had a white clapboard at Wellesley, near Boston, the interior dominated by a *quattrocento* Italian gilded and painted *cassone*. 'Oh,' she said, 'I bought that as a bargain. When it came up for auction in the sale room, the auctioneer said "no one will want this old coffin will they?" and started humming the death march from Saul, so I got it on my first low bid.'

In Boston, a key site was the Quincy Market, a classical structure of 1826 by the local architect Alexander Parris. It was being restored and converted into luxury shops and restaurants, and was the direct model for the GLC Historic Buildings Division's scheme for Covent Garden Market as a similar tourist destination. I had ample professional reasons, therefore, behind my travels in

America, it was not all social recreation, and I could hardly ignore the contemporary independence celebrations everywhere. From Boston, we visited the battle field at Concord where was fired the shot that was 'heard round the world' at North Bridge, opening the War of Independence in 1775. The memorial to the British soldiers killed (probably Hessian mercenaries, but let that pass) was deeply moving with its epitaph inscribed in granite:

> 'They came three thousand miles and died
> To keep the past upon its throne'

From James Russell Lowell's 1849 poem. I made there a solemn vow that I would devote my life to keeping 'the past upon its throne', a dedication I have pursued unswervingly for nearly fifty years.

My 1976 American visit concentrated on the East Coast between Boston and Annapolis, and that remained my main trans-Atlantic stomping ground. I tended to go to the States every year in the two decades after, and in retrospect the visits meld into one another; though my travels were extended to north, south and west, though never to the West Coast which remains *terra incognita*. Unlike stout Cortez, I have not gazed on the Pacific. Asking Fran in Massachusetts if she had ever been to San Francisco, she replied: 'Heavens, no. Why should I go there, it is quicker to fly to London.' My furthest journey was to the mid-west: Houston, Texas, and Tulsa, Oklahoma. At the latter, I met the paramount chief of the Cherokees. Disappointingly, he was dressed in a suit and tie, rather than the full panoply, war bonnet and all, but he gave me a white glass 'bears' teeth' necklace. 'When you wear this, it will help you to tell the truth.' Obviously, therefore, I never wear it; I hung it round the neck of a copy of the Portland Vase, in my cabinet of curiosities.

There was a vague Scottish connection with Oklahoma. Sir William Steuart, 7th Bart, (1795-1871), a fascinating forebear, not ancestor, of my school contemporaries Wattie Steuart Fothringham and Henry Steuart Fothringham, and their elder brother Robert of Murthly Castle, Perthshire, had travelled to Oklahoma in the 1830s after a military career which had seen action at Waterloo. Steuart was a patron of the artists Alfred Miller and George Catlin who recorded the Plains Indians in their native territory, and many of whose paintings are now in the Gilcrease Museum in Tulsa.

One result of Steuart's travels was the introduction of American buffalo to Britain. He brought them back from Oklahoma and established them on the estate at Murthly in the mid-nineteenth century where they bred successfully. They came with two Red Indian keepers who were housed in an authentic hut at Rohallion, which still survives. The buffaloes had to be banished after they killed the postman, and moved south from Perthshire to Woburn Abbey and the Duke of Bedford's private zoo, where presumably the postman was more wary of large animals. Sir William also brought back from the wilds a Cree Indian 'valet' with whom he lived happily in Scotland for ten years, an emotional man-to-man relationship he described in two autobiographical novels. Sir William's son, Will Drummond Steuart, was as unusual as his father whom he predeceased. He, too, was a soldier winning the V.C. at Lucknow during the Indian Mutiny, but died accidentally when attempting a sword-swallowing trick while drunk.

On several other forays across the Atlantic in the future, I visited and stayed with Bill Kuhn, the historian, who lectured then at a university near Evansville, Illinois, where the students were so simple, they had never been in an elevator before coming to 'college'. While Bill was incubating learning in not very bright minds, I used to go into the city by train on my own and continue round and round the Loop, the elevated central railway, which was a mesmerising pastime, staring from antique iron viaducts into first and second floor office windows at people glued to identical screens and files working at ... one wonders what?

Chicago is to Modern architecture what Rome is to the Baroque. Twentieth century Modern architecture evolved there, with the Chicago School and the first steel-framed skyscrapers, before

New York, in the work of Louis Sullivan and Daniel Burnam after the Great Chicago Fire of 1871, and the inventive suburban houses of Frank Lloyd Wright (whose signature is scratched on the mirror we used to admire in the 'Bride of Denmark' in Queen Anne's Gate). A later phase of modernism after the Second World War had left a further strata of impressive buildings in the sleek American 'International Style' pioneered at the Illinois Institute of Technology (IIT) by the German immigrant Mies van der Rohe. The development of tubular steel frames made possible very tall buildings. The Miesian Sears (now Willis) Tower in Chicago, completed in 1974, and so new when I saw it, was the tallest building in the world until 1998.

It is, however arguable that the late-twentieth century, and worse the twenty-first century craze for facile, super-tall commercial buildings has caused urban barbarism across the globe, especially in the Middle East and Asia. They are the architectural equivalent of the nuclear bomb. Just because one can do, doesn't mean one should. It is time to promote a new cult for a worldwide hundred-foot height limit, such as existed in London until it was abolished by the philistine Macmillan government in 1963. Until that date, the height limit was a statutory requirement of the LCC Fire Brigade, and as the Ronan Point explosion and the Grenfell Tower fire subsequently demonstrated, a sensible one for residential flats.

In Chicago, the sky-line of the last hundred years is, however, a thrilling creation, especially as seen from a boat on Lake Michigan. The Great Lakes were one of the surprises. I had imagined I would be able to see Canada ('friendly giant to the north') on the other side across the water, like Birkenhead from Liverpool. The boundless freshwater ocean was a startling encounter. I have never managed to get my head round the inhuman scale of America, both natural and man-made. It is vertiginous. The only way I can comprehend the size of the Great Lakes is to remember that they are not Windermere or Coniston but equal in size to the total land area of the British Isles, which are bigger than we pretend—'our little island home'—being one of the most extensive archipelagos of islands in the world. The Great Lakes are a watery inverse archipelago.

Later visits to America have often revolved around lecture tours based on the most recent book, organised by the likes of the Royal Oak Foundation (the American friends of the National Trust) or the American College of Arms Foundation (which raises money for the College of Arms). Once they both asked me to give a talk on the same visit. I thought, oh good, I will be able to prepare one lecture and give it twice over. One should have realised that the membership of Anglophile organisations interested in historic buildings and heraldry might overlap. To my embarrassment, they not only overlapped but were almost identical. Nothing could be done about the slides (an antique precursor to power-point), except shuffle them around a bit, but I was forced to extemporise and say something a little different to the same audience for the second occasion.

On lecture visits to New York, I sometimes stayed with Peter Laing, from Philadelphia where he had been a young stockbroker before he discovered the English eighteenth century and switched to the furniture department at Sotheby's. He showed me his native Philadelphia, with its art museum like a Greek temple, designed by the black American *beaux arts* classicist, Julian Abele, with its rooms of reconstructed English period rooms arranged by Fiske Kimball (director from the 1920s to 1955), one of the pre-war enthusiasts for all things Georgian and a pioneer of architectural preservation in America. We also visited the Arts & Crafts and neo-Georgian houses of Peter's relations along the Main Line.

Such speaking events were well organised at the American end, and were always combined with a friendly lunch or dinner for the guest-lecturer, unlike in England where local groups expected you to go to Canterbury or Scunthorpe and talk unremunerated at an inconvenient hour which precluded eating. The lecturer was not offered a small drink let alone dinner and then expected to find his way home afterwards, famished, exhausted, and bored, on broken-down, wintery, British Rail. Often the audience did not even show much enthusiasm for buying a signed copy of the magnificently fascinating book, whatever it was, which one was trying to promote. I now pretend I am very deaf and that prevents lecturing, an excuse used to decline all English lecture 'invitations'.

Not that talking to American groups was always without incident, and the audience could sometimes be unexpectedly daunting. Once in the 1990s I was giving a lecture on an aspect of the English Country House in the twentieth century at the Paul Mellon Centre for British Art, at Yale in New Haven. The Centre's building is a modern masterpiece designed by Louis Kahn and opened in 1977 with expensive interiors of travertine marble and white oak, with a sophisticated lecture hall on a scale more ambitious than an amateur speaker like me is used to. The audience was packed with highly intelligent students and professors who when asked at the end if they had 'any questions for the lecturer', instead of routine queries about something simple like astragals and architraves, immediately started seeking my views on political reform of the House of Lords. It was a natural jump, I suppose, from country houses to their owners. Legislative change was in the news because of the Blair plans for dismantling the Common Law, the United Kingdom and the British constitution, but it was not a question an architectural historian might have been expecting. Anyway, *faux de mieux*, they were given the benefit of *my* view on Lords Reform: to reduce the house to a maximum of 450 members, comprised of 200 hereditary peers elected by the hereditaries, 200 life peers elected by the lifers, and up to 50 appointed by the prime minister as he has to have some patronage, but that would include the Anglican bishops, preferably reduced from 26 to the 5 most senior, as originally proposed in 1910. This seemed to go down well, but I am not sure whether the audience realised it had no more foundation than anything they might have made up themselves. It seemed a far too sensible and historically sensitive solution to be taken seriously.

On another occasion in New York, when talking on a Saturday morning to a group of specialists, connoisseurs and collectors, there was a mishap. The event had been arranged in the tasteful premises of a very smart purveyor of art and antiques in Maddison Avenue, crammed with treasures and lots of Ming and Ping displayed around the gallery. The recondite, luxurious setting and the rarity of the works of art on show was all part of the *special occasion*. Everyone was solemnly admonished to take extra care, not to touch anything and keep a respectful distance, as the items on display were all very rare and 'priceless'. This created a suitably nerve-wracking atmosphere. Everyone behaved well, nobody handled anything or knocked anything over. At the end of the lecture, just as we were inhaling a nervous breath of relief, the reverberations from the polite applause caused an Imperial Ming Mutton Fat Jade Sceptre to ease slowly off its rosewood perch and smash into pieces before our horrified gaze. The organizers' faces went white; the gallery proprietor fainted; and I was hurried by my minder from the scene of disaster to lunch at the Knickerbocker Club—like a child being hastily removed from a fatal traffic accident. I never heard the sequel. Was the jade sceptre insured? Or was it just glued together again and sold on to an avid Chinese collector? I often wonder.

From the luxury shops of Maddison Avenue, to the austerities of communism, my first visit to Russia was in 1974, two years before I went for the first time to the United States. I travelled to Russia three times before the fall of communism, and in some ways preferred it then to modern klepto-oligarch Russia. There was no traffic, no advertising, no visible crime, the palaces were well looked after. One was seeing it towards the end of the regime, and for a tourist there was a certain amount of leeway for bad behaviour. The unexpected Russian sense of humour helped. It was a bit like being in a mad tyrannical prep school run by sadistic masters, but one could get by as a foreigner, if one affected to obey the rules.

The 1974 visit was part of a cruise on a Russian boat around the Baltic, which took in several cities one wanted to visit without necessarily exploring the hinterland, like Copenhagen and Helsinki which are both best approached from the sea as they have glorious harbours. The aim was to see the neo-classical Baltic capitals, St Petersburg above all, following the spectacular *Age of Neo-Classicism* exhibition at the Royal Academy, London, in 1972 where they had starred, and which was one of the most beautiful, informative and inspiring art shows of that era. It was the last of the ambitious post-war Council of Europe cultural exhibitions in different European cities from the 1950s onwards.

The Russian cruise was partly the brainchild of Sarah Griffin, a friend who had typed my D.Phil thesis at Oxford, and also included Judy Langton-Lockton, an old friend from St Andrews, and a couple of others. Sarah conceived the boat journey and organised the trip. I have never met anyone else who has been on, or even heard of, a Communist-era Russian cruise in the Baltic, so it is not clear how Sarah got the idea. She had studied Russian at university and spoke the language a bit, which helped but not that much, as in those days visitors were straitly herded and supervised by Intourist guides from the communist state travel agency whose staff spoke English and existed mainly to prevent contact with the general population.

The idea of taking a boat may have been the product of Sarah's naval background. Her father, Sir Anthony Griffin, was an admiral and Elder Brother of Trinity House, Controller of the Navy, Third Sea Lord, and finally chairman of the nationalised British Ship Building Company in the 1970s. He was a strong proponent of the sea and maritime interests to British life. As Controller of the Navy, he was responsible for creating the streamed-down model for the British fleet devised in the 1960s with an emphasis on submarines and new classes of frigates, which has lasted to the present. A proposal for large new aircraft carriers essential for joint-force-activity was proposed in the '60s but could not be afforded then, and the carriers were only built in the early twenty-first century. Sarah's idea of going to Russia by sea, rather than air, may therefore have derived from her father and his professional interests and enthusiasms.

We were glad we did. A Russian Baltic cruise was rather a good idea, as the boat sailed itself, was more-or-less punctual, had decent enough food and basic accommodation, and was gloriously drunken from early morning to night. Mine was a hard-drinking family—two uncles died of alcoholism—but even I was a little surprised by the quantities of vodka consumed by the crew. The boat was almost comfortable, compared to 'modern' concrete Intourist hotels in Russia itself, with their terrible food of the 'not-boiled' egg variety, and knitting babushkas on every landing watching guests and reporting back to H.Q. We went in September 1974, leaving from Tilbury Docks and heading across the North Sea for Zealand and Copenhagen, and onwards through the Baltic to the north east.

The bar on the boat opened every day immediately after breakfast and closed at midnight; the passengers soon followed the lead of the Russian sailors and spent their days there, though more cheerily than the crew, who always looked as if drowning unimaginable sorrows. They never smiled. When we were on shore the boat and its bar remained our home-base, conveniently moored in the harbour. 1970s Copenhagen appeared to us, still with an impoverished student outlook and hamstrung by pre-Thatcher currency controls, to be expensive. Nevertheless, the city was charmingly Ruritanian with royal sentries in uniforms of blue trousers and black coats and long hair sticking out from under their bear skin helmets, lolling and strolling rather than marching around the Amalienborg palace, 'not at all like our own dear Queen's'.

The buildings were brightly coloured, the canals and pavements clean, and the low sky-line enlivened with tame herons and copper church spires. (The Hi-Rise over-development of the suburbs lay forty years in the future.) Thanks to Nelson, and the royal Navy, who had bombarded the city in1801, making necessary extensive reconstruction, and the even more damaging British attack with phosphor rockets (a new invention) in 1807, much of Copenhagen is a beautiful early-nineteenth century neo-classical set-piece. But there is also some good early to mid-eighteenth century architecture following the plague of 1711 and fire of 1728 which destroyed the medieval town and led to the development of Frederiksstaden around the Amalienborg by King Frederick V. There are also admirable early-twentieth century classical buildings like the police headquarters of 1918 by H.A. Jacobsen.

The star draw was the early-nineteenth century work by the Danish 'Golden Age' architects C.F. Hansen and Gottlieb Bindesbøll. The biggest attraction was Bindesbøll's Thorwaldsen Museum, dedicated to the famous sculptor with all the plaster *bozzetti* for the work created by him in a lifetime in Rome. It is one of the finest neo-classical museums in Europe, comparable architecturally with the Alte Museum in Berlin, the British Museum in London, the Glyptotek in Munich, the Braccio Nuova in the Vatican, or the 6th Duke of Devonshire's Sculpture Gallery at Chatsworth. The attic forms are enlivened by Egyptian touches—palms and Nile crocodiles—and Pompeian polychromy, inside and out. The galleries with *grotteschi* decoration are arranged around a central enclosed courtyard or peristyle with Thorwaldsen's grave in the centre.

The building was conceived as much as a mausoleum and national monument as a conventional art gallery, and retains its original character to a remarkable degree. It was planned as early as the 1830s, a decade before the great sculptor's death in 1844 when he was buried within the completed building. It really celebrated his homecoming to Copenhagen from Rome. He had been a pupil of Antonio Canova and stayed on, spending all his working life in the Eternal City. There he established an international reputation and was especially popular with English collectors. Many monuments, busts and statues by Thorwaldsen embellish British houses, livery halls and churches, including a bust of Walter Scott in the Scottish National Gallery in Edinburgh and the statue of Byron in the chapel at Trinity College, Cambridge. The Marbles in the Thorwaldsen Museum today, which augment the original plasters, were mainly acquired in the twentieth century from English collections such as Thomas Hope's at the Deepdene when that was sold in 1918. As well as the formal sculpture galleries, the museum contains rooms furnished with Thorwaldsen's own Danish Biedermeier chairs and tables, and his personal collection of contemporary Danish Gold Age paintings by the likes of Jürgen Sonne and Johan Christian Dahl, and romantic classicists working in Rome like Franz Ludwig Catel. Of the sculpture, I especially admired Thorwaldsen's roundels of the Four Seasons, the model for the tomb of Bethman Hollweg, and the Shepherd Boy of which a marble version is in the Drapers Hall in London.

In 1974 the Thorwaldsen Museum was a revelation and a model of authentic museum display to aspire to. It was miraculously intact compared to the British Museum with the latters mutilated architecture and galleries painted suicide grey (which still persist), or the National Gallery with 1960s plastic egg crate false ceilings, dirty pink carpet and pale dingy painted walls. (Happily at the NG, all is since restored to Victorian splendour with silk damask, stencilling and gilding). One reason the Royal Academy Exhibition in 1972 made such an impact was because the setting had been designed in an informed and sympathetic manner with strong neo-classical colours on the walls. The sculpture displays there had been organised by John Kenworthy-Browne who became a friend and has been an influence over the years on my sculptural taste as well as introducing me to a generation of now dead scholars and aesthetes, such as Jim Lees-Milne, Pat Trevor-Roper, John Pope-Hennessy, who seemed even then like relics from a legendary era, the 'Crichel Boys'. One wondered if hyphenated names were compulsory at the Kenworthy-Browne dinner table.

'The Pope' had a distinctive high-pitched voice which Homan Potterton (a distant cousin by marriage of mine) who I met at those 1970s parties in John's Hollywood Road house, told me was modelled on that of Yeats. If so, it made a historical witness akin to a living version of a BBC archive voice-recording. It was like listening to Tennyson reading the *Charge of the Light Brigade* in sonorous Lincolnshire tones. Homan mischievously suggested that if we had slept with the old bachelors it would have linked us directly to the world of Bloomsbury and even Oscar Wilde, for Jim Lees-Milne had slept with Harold Nicolson who had slept with Malcolm Bullock (son-in-law of the Earl of Derby), who had slept with almost everyone in the Edwardian period and, Bob's your uncle, there you were in apostolic succession to the Victorian queerage.

John Pope Hennessy's Latin memorial requiem in England after his death in Florence was at the Brompton Oratory and taken by the Provost Fr Michael Scott Napier who was a friend of Pope-Hennessy's and other art historians. Fr Michael had done his national service with the decorator David Hicks and the architect Roderick Gradidge who later pioneered wearing an earring, tattoos, a pig-tail and an 'English' kilt. Only the latter did not take off as a popular male fashion. It seemed an unlikely combination, at odds with the priest's stern, ancestral military demeanour. In his address at the requiem, Fr Napier compared Pope-Hennessy's religious faith to a 'solid cushion' which struck some as an unfortunate analogy, conjuring up an image of the deceased scholar perched like Miss Moffat on a plump tuffet.

Fr Michael himself was strongly interested in architecture and had been one of Alfred Gilbey's converts at Cambridge. Michael bequeathed to me a complete set of the historic house articles in *Country Life* which he and his father (an army officer) had cut out and preserved in bound volumes from the 1920s to the 1980s. I should have continued the tradition but I haven't; I have only kept those I have written myself since the 1970s. As we walked away once after dinner at the Athenaeum (his club and mine, too, for a year, having been put up by Julian Fellowes's father Peregrine), Michael said to me, 'I don't know when I am going to die, but when I do, I would like you to have my *Country Life* albums.' The bequest came sooner than I expected, for he died too soon and had a heart attack while still in his sixties. His *Country Lifes* fill a shelf in the library at Barbon and are a delight to leaf through, as well as being a memento of a good and cultivated man.

Fr Michael saved my Catholic Faith, for the Oratory where he, through a combination of strength of character and intelligence, preserved the traditional Latin liturgy and adapted it to the reforms after the Second Vatican Council, seemed an ideal *via media*, such as the English Benedictines could have achieved but failed to do. It enabled me to carry on practising in London without grinding my teeth at having to take part in religious services that resembled a 'social' in a suburban old folks' home, as is so often the case in English churches. Dentistry is so expensive.

From Copenhagen, we continued our vodka-fuelled way through the Baltic to Finland and Helsinki, which has a terrific approach to the harbour through fortified rocky islands. The city looks its best from the sea with spires and domes, the splendid waterfront, Senators Square, the domed classical cathedral (Lutheran) on the central axis, raised up on a plinth and approached by an enormous flight of steps, flanked by symmetrical, colour-washed, neo-classical buildings. Off to one side, disturbing the symmetry, is a mad red brick Russian Orthodox Church topped with copper onions, looking like a stray from Moscow and a reminder of nineteenth century Tsarist rule as Archdukes of Finland. The first impact of that theatrical classical urban set-piece as experienced from the harbour is almost everything, though there are some good Arts and Crafts houses and the excellently designed railway station. The rest of the town on close inspection seemed grim and dull—later nineteenth century and twentieth century buildings, and sprawling post-war suburbs. The population also seemed grim. An air of northern alcoholic unhappiness pervaded and was very noticeable in the 1970s. The nearer to Russia and the Arctic, the more miserable and depressed everyone seemed to become. One could almost measure the depression level on a Richter Scale, by the latitude to the north east, reaching the depths in communist Leningrad, as St Petersburg had become after the revolution, not that we ever called it that, nor did most of its population.

We had imagined our ship would sail directly into St Petersburg and moor alongside a granite embankment with Egyptian sphinxes, porphyry obelisks and gilded chains looped through the mouths of bronze lions' heads. The harbours of Copenhagen and Helsinki had raised high the expectations of arrival in the harbour of the greatest neo-classical city of them all. Nothing had prepared us for the full horror of the sea approach from the Gulf of Finland. St Petersburg is inland in the mud flats, not directly on the Baltic. In place of the expected great estuary opening into the Neva, a concreted canalised approach cut straitly through grim derelict blackness, lined with failed industrial ancientness, scrap heaps, slums, toxic chimneys and all the desperate polluted residue of the Marxist era. Even the sky seemed gloomy and depressed. But it is worth braving the awful approach when you get there.

The giant scale defies expectation; the breadth of the river; the colossal size of the palaces and public buildings, like the vast hemicycle of the General Staff Building opposite the Winter Palace. Everything is vaster than anywhere else in Europe. The streets and squares look like a series of *prix de Rome* drawings come to life. St Petersburg makes Helsinki look like a small colonial centre. Full-scale Tsarist splendour takes the breath away, and is enhanced by the charming colours of the buildings which are painted in a dazzling range of pistachio greens, russet reds, apricot, cerulean blue ... Much of this 'authentic colouring' dates from the restoration ordered by Stalin after the destructive German siege in the Second World War, when a quarter of the city's fabric was destroyed and a similar proportion of the population died. The reconstruction and restoration of the city and surrounding palaces was so well done, with almost fanatical care, that only by looking at photographs of gutted ruins and blasted shells is it possible to comprehend the scale of the German destruction between 1943 and 1945.

Whereas in England gold is used for timid picking out of details, in St Petersburg whole domes and spires are encrusted in gold leaf, like the dome of St Isaac's Cathedral or the spire of the Peter and Paul fortress. It is thrilling. The colours and the gold were intended to give life during the monochrome winter months when the ground is covered with snow and the sky is grey. That first visit was in September. It is the best month to see the former

Tsarist capital and the summer palaces in sad beautiful parks creating an illusion of English landscape amidst the flat monotonous hinterland. In autumn the northern sunlight and crisp shadows and the decaying foliage evoke nostalgia, underlining the romantic historical tragedy of it all: the peeling stucco, the tarnished gold, the dead riches, mist over the river, sunset over the infinitely vast skyline. To quote Pushkin (translated by Nabokov):

> 'Oh dismal period, visual enchantment,
> Sweet is to me thy farewell loveliness,
> I love the sumptuous withering of nature,
> The woods arrayed in gold and purple dress.'

In those days St Petersburg felt like the capital of a dead civilisation, as dead as Venice. Today it has much the same vulgarized commercial atmosphere as everywhere-else, with computer cafes and Coca Cola machines in the undercrofts of the Winter Palace, choking traffic, mass tourism, violent crime, and screaming advertisement hoardings. It remains, however, the swansong and supreme achievement of European neo-classical architecture, truly cosmopolitan as being the work of Italian, German, French and British architects, designers and gardeners, the neo-classical buildings grouped round the Winter Palace and Hermitage and along the Neva river banks—the Admiralty, the Academy, Pushkin Theatre, Rossi Street, General Staff, the Guards Barracks, the Senate House, St Isaac's Cathedral—make up an architectural ensemble far superior to anything in Paris.

The original town plan is also notable; a blend of Amsterdam with concentric canals, and Versailles with three radiating avenues, while unusually nearly all later developments have enhanced rather than damaged the grand urban concept. The clock stopped in 1917, so it seems, everything is preserved in aspic (though in fact saved by post-war preservation and reconstruction). There is something to be said for stopping at a certain point as with Florence in the sixteenth century, or Rome in 1700. London would have been wonderful if petrified in the 1850s when George IV's Metropolitan Improvements were complete and Soane's Bank of England still intact.

On the 1974 visit, the architecture struck me most, as a firm believer that Art, beautiful landscape, and historic buildings are more worthwhile than people. The former represent permanent aspirations, objective ideals and God, while humans are transient and often inadequate. I cheered inwardly when the late Henry Thorold upset the cliché-spewing bishop of Derby by booming at a meeting, 'Church buildings are FAR more important than people!' But I was fascinated and moved by the grey, frayed, down-trodden, gloom-and-drink sodden Russian population. Communist control still seemed total in the mid-1970s. If you smiled at or talked to a waitress, a tap on her arm or a glance would lead to her instant disappearance, I hope not to Siberia. There was little of the contact which was possible on later visits when the iron claws had retracted a little. There was an air of sad resignation in the queues and half empty streets. All the civilians were shabbily dressed and looked worn and aged, but the ubiquitous bands of soldiers, sailors and military cadets wore smart uniforms of multi neo-Tsarist kinds (restored by Stalin in 1944). They seemed very young with their shaven fair hair, round pink faces and Slavic snub noses. Is this what the armies that raped and pillaged Prussia and Berlin thirty years earlier in 1945 looked like?

There were gleams and sparks of civilisation. The opera and ballet were glorious, and gloriously old-fashioned with beautiful sets and colourful costumes, unlike the depressing grisaille sets and clichéd Nazi uniforms in western opera houses, from the 1970s onwards, which made it impossible to interest the young—like nieces or godchildren—in the opera in London for it was impossible for them to follow if the golden tarnhelm had been transmuted into a plastic television set. Russian interest in culture seemed to be genuine and not just a form of communist Potemkin village. The Hermitage was full of Russian families with young children at the weekends looking at Rembrandts and Van Dycks. In the palaces and gardens at Tsarskoe Selo there was a sense of popular artistic appreciation; and something like genuine communal respect and shared ownership prevailed.

One has always relished the story of how the summer palaces—Peterhof, Tsarskoe Selo, Pavlovsk and the others—were saved after the revolution in 1917. The section of the Lord Chamberlain's department responsible for the upkeep of the palaces understanding the political situation and led by Prince George Loukomski transformed themselves overnight from courtiers into art curators. They encouraged various members of the imperial family who were still living oblivious of gathering horrors in different palaces, to escape south away from the Red Army towards the Crimea. This included the empress-dowager Maria Feodorovna, mother of Nicholas II and sister of Queen Alexandra. The dowager's favourite residence was the Cottage Palace at Peterhof though she lived latterly mainly in Kiev as she couldn't stand her daughter-in-law, and Rasputin. After the Revolution, she travelled south in slow stages to Sebastapol and safety, with fifty loads of luggage, her daughter the Grand Duchess Xenia, five grandsons, six dogs and a canary. They were rescued in 1919 by the British warship HMS Marlborough sent to the Black Sea by her nephew George V just as the Red Army closed in on the peninsular.

Meanwhile the ex-Lord Chamberlain's officials got the train to Tsarskoe Selo, determined to save the palaces from looting and ruin, and on their own initiative, turned them into State Museums. They rearranged the rooms at Pavlovsk, Tsarskoe Selo and Peterhof to their historic appearance, weeding out all the junk, photographs, plaster casts of children's hands, bibelots, and bric-à-brac, amidst which nineteenth century royalty liked to nest, and then declared the palaces and parks open to the public, the next Sunday.

They worried about the impact of heavy peasant feet on the polished parquetry floors, the product of a particularly fine Russian craft, and had a brainwave. They cut up all the felt drugget from servants' rooms and back stairs and made them into impromptu overshoes or slippers which the visitors were required to wear.

This proved the secret of success. The 'proletariat' loved the overshoes and sliding over the floors; the carpet slippers gave them a special sense of possession. By the time the Leninist authorities discovered what was going on, it was too late. They were faced by a *fait accompli*. The palaces had become State Museums, the property of the Russian People whose 'ancestors had built them' (a bit of an exaggeration as most of the skilled craftsmen, artists, gardeners and architects were immigrants from elsewhere in Europe), and everybody loved going to them and donning carpet slippers to glide round the gilded apartments. The overshoes became an established practice, and are still compulsory for visitors to the Russian palaces.

Loukomski and his colleagues continued as curators until 1926 when the darkening of the political situation forced them to emigrate to America where Loukomski taught Russian art and published several books on Russian Palace architecture in the 1940s, to celebrate the wartime alliance between Stalin and Roosevelt, when the two leaders connived to hand Eastern Europe to communist control, against Churchill's wishes.

In the Russian streets in 1974 people would beg little things and, fore-warned, we had brought a stock of biros to give out as we were told they were in short supply. Concurrent advice to 'take one's own bath plug because there weren't any' proved to be 'fake news'. People would approach and stroke one's old coat or moth-eaten jersey with a sense of wonder as if they had never seen anything so fine before. Such incidents underlined the grey tragic sadness of it all. Other encounters which tugged the heart strings were when 'students', seeing that one was British, would come up furtively to practice a little English which they had taught themselves from reading Dickens (allowed because of the pictures of Victorian 'capitalist' poverty). And listening to the BBC World Service (not allowed). Their self-taught English was good, much better than most Londoners, as it was grammatical and well-pronounced, but pointless as there was no opportunity for them to use it, but I suppose it gave them a sense of contact with the prohibited outer world.

A cheering aspect of a visit to St Petersburg seven years later in April 1981, when the cracks were developing, was that the student-types were less cowed and reticent. They not just practised a few English sentences but openly hobnobbed with foreigners and changed roubles for dollars on the Nevsky Prospekt, at three times the official exchange rate. The sweeping colonnades of the Kazan Cathedral with their beautiful Corinthian columns were a favourite spot for such illicit transactions. On the 1981 visit we flew there direct from London which was quicker and soberer. The party comprised Gavin Stamp (Pilotti from *Private Eye*), Glyn Boyd Harte (the artist), Simon Rendell (typographer and printmaker) and James Miller (a director of Sotheby's). Realising the inadequacy of the diet in Intourist hotels, we brought with us a stock of fresh apples and oranges. At the airport, the dour Russian officials said we could not bring fruit into the country and they were going to confiscate it. 'Fine,' we said, in no mood to kow-tow to officialdom, and gobbled the lot in front of them while they looked on aghast, stunned. 'We are not now bringing it in.' I feel retrospectively penitent. The fruit would have meant a lot to them in the circumstances, we should have let them have it.

The snow was melting but the temperature was still 30°F below freezing. The surrounding landscape was part snow and part mud, grey and dun coloured. There was an extraordinary experience when visiting Pavlovsk, my favourite Russian Palace, situated in a park like Stowe. It was built for mad Tsar Paul to the designs of Charles Cameron, an architect of interest to me, and the Italian Vincenzo Brenna. When I arrived at Pavlovsk, it was winter. All the statues were still in their protective wooden 'sentry boxes' and the ground was a mess of frozen slush and mud. On emerging later in the morning on the other side of the palace after an extensive tour, Spring had arrived. The statues had emerged from their covers, the ground as far as the eye could see had been swept with birch brooms, the gravel raked, the urns and flower beds filled with flowering plants from the glass houses. The sun shone briefly. The transformation was staggering, the season had been changed at the flick of a trowel.

Tyranny with thousands of human hands at its disposal can move mountains. This gardening feat reminded me of a less benevolent story of wonders worked by tyranny, related to me by Matthew Festing about his father, the Field Marshal. Matthew's father had been Commander of British Forces in Hong Kong in 1945-1946, after the War, working with the mainland Chinese to mop up Japanese pockets. One day their tanks were held up by an enormous impassable rock blocking the way. The Chinese commander said, I will deal with this. Leave it to me. He organised a battalion of ant-like Chinese soldiers with shovels to dig a huge hole in the ground for the rock to subside into, and in due course the tanks rolled over it and continued onwards. The British were most impressed and said to their Chinese counterpart, 'That was a brilliant job, can we thank your men for their amazing effort?' 'No,' said the Chinese general, 'you can't, they are underneath the rock.'

In St Petersburg we got drunk every evening and behaved badly. Champagne from Georgia was so cheap, and vodka so plentiful it was difficult not to. There was even a little bar, selling Georgian champagne and vodka, concealed by a curtain, in an alcove off the Jordan Staircase in the Winter Palace. I fell down the mile-long escalator on the underground while admiring Stalin's classical decoration: the huge chandeliers, the gilt bronze Piranesian candelabra, and the marble and mosaic vistas. At one 'Pektopah' the waiter refused to serve us any more vodka and champagne because he said WE were drunk, surely unique for Russia. In 1981 we were much less tied to our Intourist guides and made forays (seemingly) on our own, though we could only read two words of Russian, 'Pektopah' for restaurant and 'Boksau' for railway station. We made the most of our two words and, for instance, were able to work out the direction of underground trains from the fact that the central interchange was the Moscow Boksau, so we could tell if we were travelling inwards, or outwards into the frozen tundra. We even felt confident enough to take the local train to Tsarskoe Selo (Russia's first railway line) as we could read the

Boksau destination and could not, we hoped, be whisked off to Vladivostok or Siberia.

We visited restaurants on our own, and became a bit over-confident. One evening we found a Pektopah and decided to eat there. We went in. It was spacious but the tables were empty. There were large pretentious menus bound in gold-tooled red plastic with large tassels, and the usual lengthy Communist bill of fare which we knew from experience might mean a single dish (trout or chicken) if you were lucky. We looked forward, with hungry anticipation. Drinks were brought to us, but no food. More drinks were brought to us, but still no food. Odd single men came in and disappeared upstairs. Eventually a 'waiter' materialised and we asked for food. He burst into laughter. The penny dropped. The Pektopah was a 'front' and we had stumbled into a brothel. When in Rome ... as we were all drunk enough. A couple of our party went to explore and were not seen again that night. They said the girls were intelligent, amusing and keen to practise their English. They went home with them to a modern Communist era flat near the Finland Station and spent the whole night chatting about current affairs.

One of the reasons I wanted to re-visit St Petersburg was to study the buildings of Charles Cameron, the British eighteenth century architect who had designed new suites of rooms at Tsarskoe Selo for Catharine the Great, and the Agate Pavilion and Cameron Gallery there. I was preparing a little book about Cameron at the time, but it was never printed as the publisher Robert Oresko who had commissioned short illustrated art books from nearly everyone in London, lost his financial backer and let us all down. Oresko was a Bronx New Yorker with an obsession for the royal family of Savoy and the palaces of Turin. He was one of the more exotic figures on the fringes of London scholarly life in the 1980s. One of his disappointed authors dubbed him an 'homme fatale'. He lived in a *ménage à trois* in Bedford Gardens, Kensington, with a rich married man and the latter's intelligent teenage son. Robert thought of himself, with his snobbery and mid-Atlantic vowels, as a Society hostess for the London art world, if not the Muse of History herself. He was always at private views, and especially active in the Court History Society founded by Philip Mansel, a serious historian.

The dusty typescript and old Russian black and white, Novosti Press Agency photographs, for my Oresko Cameron book still languishes in a file. In the end, the project was overtaken by the work of a young Russian author with more access to sources at that end, who made a better job of it, though I discovered some new information about Cameron's British origins. Cameron had presented himself to Catharine the Great as a native Scot and a Jacobite, but in fact he was a Londoner born in Shepherd Market where his father was a carpenter. As the Irish used to say about the fantasist architectural historian Brian de Breffny (son of a Chiswick taxi driver): 'the pen is mightier than the fraud', so with Cameron, his designs were mightier than his fraud. His work is fascinating, like Adam on steroids, and executed in all the rich materials of the Russian empire, agate and amethyst, porphyry and strange rich marbles we called 'dazzleite', and gilded bronze, and amaranth parquetry. Cameron's interiors are a heady mix, even when sober.

I particularly wanted to see the cathedral of St Sophia built in 1785 with a centralised plan and dome, if it still existed. It had been built on the edge of the parks at Tsarskoe Selo, but did not figure in any of the 1980s tourist routes or contemporary guidebooks. There was a distinct possibility that it had been destroyed in the Second World War. Discovering it was one of those thrilling personal moments that sometimes reward the assiduous historian. After the Revolution in 1917, the small planned model town of which it was the centrepiece had become a military camp, and barracks were not visitable by foreigners or shown on modern maps and plans. I was determined to try to find it, if I could. From the raised terrace of the Cameron gallery at one end of the great palace, I scanned the distant skyline on the side away from the railway station which my innate (pre-sat-nav) topographical sense told me might be the right direction. Lo, there was Cameron's dome, recognisable from ancient photographs, some distance away above the boundary tree belt on the far side of the artificial lake in the Catharine Park. We set off in that direction. Distances are always further than you think, such is the scale of Tsarist Russia. But a little gate in the park wall eventually led to the barracks area. (One wondered if it was the place where a solitary sentry had stood every day up to 1917, when the order was rescinded, guarding a snow drop that Catharine had noticed in 1780.)

On the other side of the gate in the outer world, there the cathedral stood, overlooking an unused military exercise field. The dome was intact but the building generally was in a sorry state. It was semi-gutted having been shelled in the siege and not restored after the war. The interior, with granite columns, gilded capitals and coffered plasterwork, had been destroyed by the Germans. The outer walls were still scarred and pockmarked by shells and bullets; scrubby bushes and sapling trees engulfed the shattered walls. There was a sinister atmosphere. How many must have been killed there?

Suddenly, a wild Dostoyevskian figure in rags with a long matted beard emerged from the crypt and started gesticulating and shouting, waving his emaciated arms towards the ruin. At first we thought he was a madman, but then realised he was talking about the building, for his incomprehensible Russian sentences were punctuated by the word 'Cameron'. This was amazing. One could not imagine a tramp, for instance, in the derelict ruins of neo-classical Liverpool being able to expatiate on the work of James Wyatt, John Foster, Joseph Gandy, Harvey Lonsdale Elmes, or C.R. Cockerell. Reflecting later, it seemed perhaps he may have been an Orthodox priest, squatting secretly in the war-damaged wreck of his church, who had emerged to explain its history to unexpected visitors.

Russia was not the only Communist country visited at that time. My first visit to Prague also took place in 1981 and was organised by my colleague at Historic Buildings, Jonathan Balkind. With characteristic chutzpah, Jonathan wrote on GLC paper to the

Prague historic buildings office and said we were an official visit from their London equivalent, coming on a fraternal, cultural trip to compare preservation philosophies and practical approaches. It worked, and we were invited to meet some of their officials and visit various sites. One wonders if the well-known Marxist sympathies of the LCC and GLC Architects Department, may have helped open that door. (The LCC had gone over to building pre-fabricated concrete flats two weeks after the Communists in Russia had ditched Stalin's classical architectural tastes and gone over to Hi-Rise 'Modern' concrete housing.)

When it came to accommodation, we were still the pawns of Cedok, the local tourist office. Cedok was a good match for Intourist in Russia, and booked us into the most expensive hotel in town, opposite the Smetana Theatre. The bedrooms were hideously pretentious and dowdy. The visitor was mesmerised by the naff Woolworth's-looking white and gold wallpaper in the bedrooms. On close inspection, it turned out to be hand painted to *look* like real printed wallpaper, such were the exigencies of failed Communist economics. The fourth wall was covered with crazy paving. We tried to move to another more *simpatico* place, the Hotel Paris, but the receptionist there immediately rang Cedok and we had to return, tails between our legs, to the berth allocated chez Smetana. We did attend a Smetana opera in the red plush and gilt theatre, but the music was not memorable.

Jonathan and I took Paul Draper, the architectural draughtsman, then a 'struggling artist' but now prosperous from his Anglo-Swiss Bisque, central heating radiator business. The idea was that he would sketch the Baroque architecture, a rather Grand Tour arrangement. His ink drawing of the eagle doorcase on the Thun-Hohenstein Palace in Prague hangs framed on the staircase wall at Barbon. It is a memento of the enjoyably various baroque

Opposite: Baroque doorcase of the Clam Galas Palace in Prague. Drawn by Paul Draper who accompanied Jonathan Balkind and JMR as Grand Tour artist in the party.1981.

Clam-Gallasův palác. Praha.

doorcases of Prague with their split pediments, heraldry, caryatids, terms, fierce beasts, face masks and seemingly limitless variations of sculptural virtuosity. The first evening we escaped from the dud hotel and explored the old town in the gloom, for there was a welcome lack of street lighting, and the absence of bright illumination enhanced the antique appeal. It was as if nothing had been touched since 1750. There is no comparable architectural panorama anywhere. The seemingly infinite vistas of baroque and gothic buildings and pavements with cobble mosaics in black and white patterns stretch from Old Town Square through the labyrinthine lanes around the Clementinum, across the Charles Bridge with gesticulating Counter-Reformation saints, the silhouette of Great St Nicholas, past the Plague Monument, like all those throughout the Holy Roman Empire in the form of a grotto-esque *guglio* or obelisk with Our Lady on top, and then Mala Strana and the climb up hill to the orgasmic climax of the Square in front of the cathedral, archbishop's palace and the castle.

It was all enchanting in its dark splendour, with no floodlighting, no illuminated advertisements, no light pollution, chiefly the stars, just glorious chiaroscuro. All seemed so dreamlike, we thought it would not be there the next day, a not uncommon reaction as many find Prague's architecture an incredible fantasy. A reviewer of *Operation Daybreak*, the romanticised 1975 film about the assassination of SS Obergruppenführer Reinhard Heydrich, Reichsprotector of Bohemia, with Anthony Andrews pretending to be the Slavic hero, caught this aspect when he wrote ironically, 'how good to see reality filmed in a setting of fantasy'. It showed the city exactly, for it was filmed on location. It was one of those films where you can tell the goodies—they were all beautiful—and the baddies because they had harsh German accents. I thought it was terrific, with its haunting music by David Hentschel.

The arrangements with the Czech Ministry worked, and we met intelligent, interesting people, none of them Party members and all sharing a distrust and suspicion of the regime. For a visitor, the obstacles to freedom seemed intermittent and inconsistent compared to Russia. The principal one for inhabitants was the embargo on foreign travel. The population seemed western with attractive if small flats and were dressed relatively well, *à l'Americaine* in jeans. In the countryside they owned their own houses, and there were some semblances of a free economy; it was possible to buy fruit for cash from the orchards of farms. We escaped as soon as we could from the Smetana Hotel and decamped to the country where we found a friendly little hotel at Revnice, commuting into the city by train.

Prague had not been damaged in the war, nor by the communists, there had even been good restoration work over the previous quarter of a century. Although Czechoslovakia was not strongly religious like Poland, the cathedral was magnificent and still used for worship in the absence of the archbishop who had been expelled. His empty palace was intact, the state rooms lined with mid-eighteenth century Gobelin *Nouvel Indes* tapestries, similar to those at Pavlovsk in Russia or the set at Arundel Castle which had been bought by the 9th Duchess of Norfolk direct from the manufactory in Paris for £9 a yard in 1750.

The superb late-Gothic architecture of the cathedral with Baroque fittings makes the ideal aesthetic combination. Bohemian Gothic is the only European later medieval development of the style which can compare in quality and originality with English Perpendicular. The huge silver shrine of St John Nepomuk, hero of the Jesuit counter-reformation, is situated off centre in the ambulatory, just like an eighteenth century state coach which had stopped to allow Cinderella in her glass slippers to descend into the cathedral choir. To our astonishment, a new series of stained glass windows were being installed in the cathedral in the communist 1980s.

Apart from the architecture of Prague, I most appreciated the warm, vaulted beer cellars which were full of 'students and artisans', the compulsory light opera mix, and which sold very good, very cheap beer. You just kept ordering, and the waiters put a pencil tick for each pint consumed on a piece of paper on your table. At the end they added up the ticks, and you paid before leaving. By the end of the evening, the paper was black with pencil strokes.

At our favourite bar in Mala Strana, we met a group of Czechs our own age who had a jazz band. They were incredibly kind to us. On our last day we had to catch an early morning flight to London, so had come back into Prague from Revnice to be in time to catch the plane. Cedok, who obviously hated us, said there were no hotel rooms available. It looked like a night under the gas lamps and stars. We were laughing at our predicament to one of the jazz musicians. He said, 'but you must come and stay with my family'. We accepted the kind invitation with alacrity, as the nights in Prague in the autumn can be cold.

Their flat was very compact. I suspect our friend and his family had given up their own beds for us and slept on the kitchen floor. They were exceptionally, almost biblically, generous to strangers, and brave; entertaining foreigners at home was of course against the communist rules. I often think of them and hope they had a wonderful life after the Velvet Revolution and the fall of communist oppression. We posted them a little thank-you but never heard from them again. The holiday in Prague was one of those happy high points comparable to my birthday at St Florian in 1969, occasional moments at Civitella Ranieri, or my first term at Oxford. I had just turned twenty-six, was in love, and Prague was absolute bliss: the most beautiful buildings in the world, friends, golden autumn weather, unlimited beer ... what more does anybody need?

6

Dulce Domum

I HAVE BEEN an unconventional acquirer of houses, both in London and the country, having bought property by telegram while in Italy, through the Public Receiver from the bankruptcy court, and sight unseen from an unknown estate agent. There is no point in commissioning a surveyor's report; it will only give you reasons for *not* buying a place you like. None of my houses has fallen down and I do not know anyone whose house has fallen down in its entirety. In my early years in London I lived in rooms and little flats. In autumn 1973 when I first worked in the capital after university, writing my first two articles for *Country Life*, I lodged in a flat in Mortimer Street, north of Oxford Street, courtesy of Brian Pilkington through the good offices of a friend, Christopher Brown, who was a school contemporary of Brian's. Brian was always generous. He didn't work as he had an income from his family's glass company at St Helen's in Lancashire, and he collected art, including a group of Gainsborough drawings from Althorp (which the egregious Raine Spencer had sold surreptitiously to a London dealer); and he travelled a lot, hence his flat being available.

When I joined Christopher Brown and Anthony Turner in Dijon in summer 1974 while they were writing a guidebook on Burgundy (published by Batsford in 1977) and I was preparing an article on the Jacques Gabriel building of the *Palaces des Ducs* in Dijon for *Country Life*, Brian swept by in his white Bentley and took us all out for dinner at the *Restaurant aux Trois Faisans*, then the best in the town. Or rather, he took everybody except me who had been struck down with virulent food poisoning from a sausage sandwich in the fly-blown station bar at the railway halt near Arc et Senans in Franche Comté. I had made an arduous solitary pilgrimage to venerate Ledoux's Royal Salt Works, a neo-classical masterpiece. My virtue was definitely NOT rewarded on that occasion. I was ill for a week and missed out on all Brian's special treats.

From Mortimer Street, I moved to Canonbury Grove overlooking the New River in Islington, lodged there for a few months with the barrister and copyright expert John Mummery, now a judge, and his wife. They were newly married and expecting their first baby. A bedroom had been done up for an *au pair*, which was let pro tem, and the deal was that when the happy event occurred the tenant would make way for nanny and move out. There followed a high-up room in a tottering Georgian lodging house, seemingly in danger of falling into the Grand Union Canal on the corner of Colebrooke Row, Islington. The ground floor was a scruffy minicab office, another floor was occupied by a single female with a red light in her window. Islington was still part slum in the early 1970s, the stucco cracked, the brickwork filthy, the paint peeling, the 'railings' round the squares gardens still war-time replacement chicken wire. Now everything is smartly renovated, cast iron railings reinstated and gardens tended. Islington has been the family home of three recent prime ministers: Tony Blair, Gordon Brown and Boris Johnson, though David Cameron lived in that other inner city slum-made-good, Notting Hill.

When it looked as if the structural cracks and sagging floors in Colebrooke Row presaged imminent descent into the canal, I moved to a basement in Hampstead. Cloth Hill in The Mount, off Heath Street, was my base for eight years until 1982. There I succeeded Nicholas John, dramaturge of ENO, as the tenant. Nick and I had painted the rooms, with me helping him, but when he found he could not stand the landlady, he handed over the flat with relief to me within a year. It was my first real London home, and I occupied the basement comprising the old kitchen with a large, stone-jambed fireplace and iron range, a long brick-paved passage past the wine cellar, with a board of bells for servants, and the old housekeeper's room still complete with fireplace and a Georgian fitted wooden dresser which was used as a bookcase. The bathroom was up a flight of steps tucked in under the main stairs. The present charming American owners of the house still refer to the basement as 'John Rob's rooms'.

If people asked where one lived, the answer was, 'In a cellar in the background of *Work*'. Ford Maddox Brown's painting *Work* completed in 1865, showing navvies digging drains and fashionably dressed passers-by, depicts The Mount; and the eighteenth century railings and wrought iron lamp overthrow of Cloth Hill on the left, remain unchanged from the 1860s. The house belonged to Roger Ellis, Secretary of the Historical Manuscripts Commission (HMC), and his wife Honor who ran the Anglo-Italian Society. Roger was a scholar, expert on medieval seals, and a great help to me, reading and commenting on my manuscripts for early books and giving good advice. He proposed me for the Society of Antiquaries which was then a learned society.

Upstairs, the rooms at Cloth Hill were panelled and there was an open well staircase with turned timber bannisters, very like that at Uppark. The Ellises had painted the walls a faded pink in emulation of the pre-fire Georgian colouring in that magical National Trust house. The rooms at Cloth Hill were full of books and paintings, drawings by Romney, good rugs and Georgian furniture from both their family houses. Even when on their own, they dressed for dinner every night in the 1970s and '80s, and he chose a bottle of good claret from his cellar. The food was less good; 'the staff' were slightly mad male dailies of a type encountered in the mid-twentieth century but now extinct, probably ex-soldiers suffering from shell shock. Honor could not cook. So the delicious Médoc often accompanied beans on toast, in the panelled dining room with silver candlesticks and family portraits. Part of the deal was that the tenant should house-sit on the occasional weekends when they went away, closing the shutters and ensuring the Reynolds did not disappear. The rent was commensurately modest. I cannot remember whether it was 10 shillings a week or £10 a month, but ten came into it, and it was not in the league of modern London rents.

Roger was a fund of good stories. It was fun occasionally to dine with them, when they had guests. I met there Hugh Murray-Bailey who was the first scholar to write about the planning of baroque state apartments, and Christopher Tadgell who since has published single-handedly a massive multi-volume history of *World Architecture*, and Cecil Gould from the National Gallery (who had been proposed for the Reform by Guy Burgess and seconded by Anthony Blunt). Cecil was an expert on Venetian painting, and the godfather of the Ellis's daughter Susanna. Old Lord Harrowby, a long-serving commissioner of the HMC, also used to stay at The Mount when there were meetings in London. In his old-fashioned way, he probably thought of Hampstead as being conveniently on the way between Staffordshire where he lived at Sandon and London where the HMC meetings took place in WC1. Certainly, Cloth Hill with its library, drawing room, dining room, Mrs Ellis's sitting room, conjoined entrance and staircase halls, had some of the feel of a country house near London, rather than actually in it.

Roger told me about his fascinating war-time role, not then public knowledge. (Rather as our Historic Buildings colleague Paul Calvocoressi told us about Bletchley Park, his father Peter then being in the process of writing the first history of Enigma.) Bobby Gore, later paintings expert at the National Trust, and Roger served together in the army in Italy in 1944. Their senior commanding officers, realising that they were 'Art and Archives', put them in charge of looking after the historical treasures of Italy as the Allies fought their way northwards. When they got to Florence, they found that their opposite numbers in the German commandant's office, who had quit shortly before the British arrived, had left everything in order ready for them. All the files, and explanatory notes were laid out on the desk, with up-to-date inventories explaining where everything was. Many of the paintings were stored at Montegufoni, the Sitwell's castle in Tuscany, and the archives were in a monastery. I was told all this decades before the Americans started making self-glorifying films and claiming that they had single-handedly saved the art treasures of Italy in 'Operation Venus' at the end of the war.

I lived at The Mount for eight years and in many ways it suited me and I liked Roger and the faded country house atmosphere. My sitting room had an old rug, a couple of Victorian armchairs, a mahogany writing table, engravings, drawings and the English transfer-printed Regency china I then collected—Spode, Worcester, New Hall, Copeland, Bloor Derby. The coffee cans were used for pencils and the saucers for paper clips. The drawback was the situation in Hampstead, dependent on the Northern Line, one of the worst on the London Underground which stopped running at midnight. The only good thing about it were the passengers' contribution: the graffiti scribbled on the tunnel walls in the 1970s. 'Life is a sexually transmitted disease'. 'Drink varnish—It gives you a good finish.' 'Humpty Dumpty was pushed.' 'This wall available in paperback soon.' 'Is this what it means to be alone?' 'Wrong way round old boy.' 'Down with nineteenth century church music.' 'I wish I had not come to London'—'So do we.' They trumped those in the lavatory of the Radcliffe Camera, and supported the view that Hampstead was inhabited by intellectuals. The underground service itself was a nightmare. Often when the British Rail train into Euston or King's Cross was late, the last underground had left and it meant walking three miles up hill with my bag.

There was also a worry about health in the damp, dark basement. The rooms were below ground at the back, and everything used to go slightly mouldy; and not much light came in through the front windows because they were shaded by the ancient mulberry trees in the garden overlooking The Mount. Still, the rent was amazingly cheap, and the unspoilt eighteenth century house was civilised, Italophile, and scholarly, with an admirable *ancien regime* atmosphere.

A compromise was brokered for a time, continuing at Cloth Hill, but buying a cottage in Lancashire, accessible by train, for weekends and holidays. The idea for this had germinated from a suggestion after my grandfather died. There was an unused detached barn by the main road at Catcrag, the land we own at Witherslack near Grange-over-Sands. I was told that if planning permission to convert was forthcoming, I could have the barn for a house. This was an exciting prospect as Catcrag has happy childhood memories and interesting landscape. Architects' plans were commissioned and planning permission applied for. The area is in the Lake District National Park which, quite rightly, has strong rules against the conversion of old farm buildings. Permission was refused, went to appeal and was turned down again.

I am very pleased planning permission was refused, because I prefer the barn unconverted, and also because the road was subsequently dual-tracked to ease motorised access for urban tourists to Windermere, further unbalancing the sustainability of a fragile landscape. The barn would have been like living in a house on a motorway. I have kept the old building (*circa* 1830) unaltered, but have subsequently re-roofed it in Westmorland slate and repaired it, and let it to a succession of tenants over the years, as a stable, a wood-turning workshop, and latterly to a student from the Glasgow School of Art as 'an animation studio involving woodworking, model making, painting and filming.' (It is insured for fire). My farm tenant, Simon, does not want the barn, as it is not suitable for livestock, and too small for machinery.

The idea of the barn at Witherslack was exciting, so after failing to achieve its conversion, I wrote to the local estate agents in Grange asking them to let me know of any old cottages for sale in the area. They kept sending particulars for pebble-dashed 1930s bungalows, suitable for Darby and Joan to retire to in the balmy seaside climate of Morecambe Bay, but not what one had in mind. Then in 1976 they told me of the Manor House in Flookburgh, an interesting Grade II* listed house dating from 1686 with mullion windows and Lake District cylindrical chimneys. Pevsner had noticed it as the earliest symmetrical house with a central front door in Lancashire. It was in the village street with an attached barn and a half acre burgage plot ('Langrigg' in Scottish parlance) as a garden at the back, with flat fields beyond leading to the sea about half a mile away. It was five minutes' walk from Cark Station on the picturesque Furness Railway from Lancaster through Silverdale, Arnside and over the Kent estuary to Cark-in-Cartmel, so directly accessible with one change at Preston or Lancaster by hourly train from Euston. I was in Italy at the time and sent an offer to buy by telegram from Umbertide. It was accepted. The price was little different from that of a semi-detached bungalow.

Apart from the old house and garden, Flookburgh was an unusual place. Perhaps if I had known it better, one might not have perched there. The village contained not a single middle class person, let alone gentry; it was far removed from the pretentious suburbanising of southern English rural life, and there was hardly a car at that time. The villagers were largely fishermen, gathering cockles and Morecambe Bay shrimps from the sands, and market gardeners growing flowers and vegetables in the frost-free climate with good soil, or they had 'proper jobs', commuting by train across the Leven estuary to the Glaxo Pharmaceutical factory at Ulverston, or the shipyards, building warships and nuclear submarines at Barrow. My new neighbours were welcoming. On one side they were fishermen and I bought my shrimps directly from them. When I first arrived and was digging my new vegetable beds, a friendly face appeared over the wall with a tray of seedling cabbages and onions, and said 'would you like some plants?' On the other side were the Sadeckis. Mr Sadecki had come over from Poland to fight for the Allies during the war and stayed after the Russians stole his homeland, marrying a local girl. He had a broad Lancashire accent, and apart from his name, seemed a convincing native of Flookburgh. He used the barn for his car (a rarity in the village), and he kept an eye on the house when I was not there and did the garden for me. We remained friends and in touch after I moved away, until Mrs Sadecki died in a nursing home a decade or so later.

Flookburgh was a decayed borough rather than a village, situated on the peninsular between the Kent and Leven estuaries on the north side of Morecambe Bay. It had been given a charter by Edward I, and had a small market place with stone cross as well as a long main street lined with basically seventeenth century buildings, and even possessed some borough regalia. It had never fulfilled its early promise, but had remained alive over the centuries, being on the route across the sands of Morecambe Bay, from Lancaster to the detached Furness peninsular. The main street contained several pubs for thirsty travellers while they were on dry land, such as the Crown Inn opposite my house. The village had gone into sleepy retreat after the construction of good main roads inland in the 1830s, so though seemingly grey, gloomy and in-bred—the polite called it 'old-world'—it was not economically depressed. There were five shops including a butcher and an electrical shop selling 'white goods', as well as a general store, a chemist, and a separate post office which had succeeded my house; the manor house having served that purpose in the early-twentieth century.

The character of the place came from the fishing. Flookburgh is the centre of the Morecambe Bay shrimp industry. To call it an 'old world fishing village', as Peter Fleetwood-Hesketh did in *Murray's Guide to Lancashire*, makes it sound more picturesque than it is. Morecambe Bay shrimping is achieved by trawling the shallows and channels when the tide is out. The sea goes out twice a day, leaving 400 square miles of treacherous sands. The trawling is done with tractors dragging trailers flanked by nets. David Cox's Victorian watercolours of the bay show horse-drawn shrimping carts which were more scenic, but they had been replaced by scrap-iron tractors after the war. Salt water is destructive and the sands are dangerous; the tractors can easily be sucked in and the sea corrodes all metal, a deterrent to using smart, new equipment, so everything tended to be old, patched together and rusty. The fishermen's burgage plots behind their old houses looked more like scrap yards full of second-hand bits for broken tractors and spare wheels for trailers.

The little brown shrimps were boiled in iron wash tubs and shelled by women, wives of the fisher men at old tables in the backyards. It was a communal activity and they sat in groups, listening to the wireless and nattering together while busy fingers

The Manor House, Flookburgh, with Mr Sadecki's car parked in front. Built 1686. Sold by JMR in 1986 on its 300th birthday.

speedily stripped the tiny shells, as if knitting. It is more difficult than it looks, and I would advise never to buy unshelled shrimps as an economy, leave that to the professionals and pay extra. There were Zola-like undertones at Flookburgh. The fishermen had hereditary rights over certain channels and sand banks; if these were infringed it led to 'trouble'. There were stories of ears being bitten off in violent disputes. Outside encroachment and trespass, without tribal local knowledge of the changing tides led to death, as notoriously happened with the Chinese cocklers sent to their watery doom by Liverpool gang-masters. They were cut off and drowned by the galloping waves sweeping across the gleaming, sandy mud.

I enjoyed restoring the little white-washed manor house and planting the garden, with a central avenue of fruit trees leading from the lawn behind the house to the vegetable garden at the bottom. Glyn Boyd Harte helped me with the interior, stencilling pineapples in red and grey on the hall screen, graining the woodwork in the dining room. I painted that room a deep Pompeian shade and the sitting room spinach green, covering the floors with Chinese rush matting smelling of tea, which I bought in Ulverston. Incredibly cheap (and no doubt woven by slave labour), it proved almost indestructible and I still had portions in use after forty years.

Flookburgh suited me as a bachelor retreat for ten years, and had the atmosphere of a holiday home, if not quite seaside as the village is half a mile from the bay itself. It was a good base for going over to Catcrag for wooding and pottering, and convenient for exploring the western, less-frequented, reaches of the Lake District, like Coniston with Ruskin's house, Broughton-in-Furness with the George III jubilee obelisk, Ravenglass with a Roman harbour, and Wasdale with the most dramatic stone screes. People came to stay. I held my first party at New Year 1977, and started a tradition which outlived Flookburgh. Mary Sandys, who worked in publishing in London, was a local girl and rented a cottage from her brother, Myles, overlooking Windermere which she dubbed 'Surbiton-sur-lac'. She always had groups of her friends to stay at holiday time. Often we went to her, or they came to me, and we had a joint party around New Year, bringing our two groups together. Once doing the *place à table* in a drunken haze, I stupidly arranged my table with all her friends down one side and my guests down the other like two opposed football teams.

Some people came as individuals and stayed there when I was away, like Rory Young the sculptor, stone-carver and letterer who trained under Simon Verity in Gloucestershire. Rory made a copy of the large, traditional, stone, Lancashire fireplace in the dining room for one of his clients. Angus Taylor also stayed regularly while he was researching his history of the Kendal architects George and Francis Webster whose country house, a barge-boarded *cottage orné,* was situated up the hill at Eller Howe nearby, and whose works covered Lancashire and south Westmorland.

There were only three bedrooms at Flookburgh but that enabled me to have two or three guests to stay at a time, which was a good number to entertain, in the years when friends were still Spartan and before they married. The roof space at the top of the house, though lit by a stepped mullioned window in the central gable, was floor-less and inaccessible when I bought the place. In 1979, when I re-slated the roofs of the house and barn, I also reclaimed the top storey, putting in a staircase and a floor, and converting it into a single spacious library-study. It was the most interesting room in the house, being a late-medieval or early-Tudor crook cottage of oak which had been raised up and reconstructed as the roof of the new house when that was built in 1686. It was atmospheric and because it was high above the village street, it made a peaceful private retreat for reading, writing or just sitting. It also meant that an extra guest could be installed up there on a mattress, if necessary. Flookburgh, nicknamed 'Pineapple', symbol of hospitality, was a good northern nest for me at that stage of my life, and friends liked visiting, or so they pretended.

Meanwhile in London I decided that I needed to move from The Mount in Heath Street and to be closer in, nearer to the railway stations and the British Library (then still part of the British Museum) where I often did my research in the early evenings, after the office. The books would be ordered well ahead by telephone, using the printed catalogue, which enabled them to be brought by van to the Reading Room in Great Russell Street from Nissen huts in Woolwich Arsenal; this took several hours. The cumbersome antiquated process worked quite well if it was given enough time. I much preferred working in the old library within the museum, especially in the Edwardian North Library with its handsome, fat, black marble Doric columns, now destroyed to make way for the antiseptic white boxes beloved of a certain type of non-visual museum curator. They describe them as 'neutral', though why spaces that resemble experimentation chambers in a Nazi camp can be described as 'neutral' stumps me. I prefer marble, gilding and polychromy as a backdrop for antiquities, many of which come from temples, palaces and churches.

The new British Library was a typically wrong-headed 1960s British concept, though it took decades to design and implement, that lengthy gestation also being characteristic of British public works. Instead of building a complete new library in the St Pancras station yard, the British Library should have erected only a modern book stack there with the ability to expand the shelf area in the future (space which the new library lacks) and connected by an efficient, computerised, underground railway to the old reading rooms in Bloomsbury. That would have kept the handsome historic library interiors in use and cost a fraction of the money spent on the over-budget St Pancras project with finite book storage space and fewer seats in the reading room than the 308 spaces in the Round Reading Room at the British Museum.

The aim was to be within walking distance of the library and the station, so I focussed on Bloomsbury. My aim was to be five or ten minutes' walk from Euston, like Cark for Flookburgh at the other end. A Victorian flat in bomb-damaged Red Lion Square would have done and I was considering it seriously when my historic buildings colleague, Martin Andrews told me that several buildings opposite his house in Doughty Mews were coming up for sale. They belonged to Collins, a firm of printers based at 12 Doughty Street, who used them for storage and garages for vans, with the odd sitting tenant upstairs.

The printing firm had gone bankrupt during the 1982 recession, and all Collins's property was being sold off by the Public Receiver. The arrangement was that sealed bids in envelopes had to be submitted by a certain date. Lady Ash, the American wife of Sir Eric Ash, Rector of Imperial College in Kensington, and treasurer of the Royal Society, was known to be buying them as an investment, and a home for her architect daughter Cany (who also worked in the GLC's Architects Department) and her husband Robert Sakula who had been the last amanuensis of Clough Williams-Ellis. I did not have much hope with such opposition, but I put in a bid for No. 8. To my surprise, it was accepted. Lady Ash secured four or five others, and Robert and Cany converted and moved into one, and have been my neighbours for thirty-eight years, running their award-winning practice from the mews.

I found myself the owner of a derelict garage behind Doughty Street. It needed re-roofing, new windows, electric wiring, plumbing, a bathroom, a kitchen. Martin opposite, being an architect and on the spot in Doughty Mews, did the drawings for me, and somehow, I found an Irish builder from south east London, John Hands, who assembled a little team of unreliable workmen.

The conversion from garage to house proceeded at its own pace, though not without the infuriating delays that all London building projects seem to entail when the contractor disappears for days on end at crucial moments, and timetables become fictional fantasies. One day, the site was like a Marie Celeste scene with all the signs of work in progress and tools scattered around as if in use, but no builders. There was blood on the concrete floor beside a new drain. Scenes of death, murderous brawls or worse floated across my mind. It turned out not to be that serious. The boy working on the manhole cover had cut himself badly and they had all gone to A&E, but soon returned with the victim neatly plastered and the proud possessor of forty stitches. The work took a year to complete. More trouble came from my neighbour's builders than my own; their incompetence damaged my new roof to such an extent that I had to rebuild it totally twenty years later, and they caused a flood spoiling the new interior, and nearly killing me with stress and rage at a difficult moment when I was also being sued for libel.

Carried away with the excitement of a successful purchase from the receivers-in-bankruptcy, and underestimating the building time, I had given notice on my Georgian cellar in The Mount, so needed somewhere to stay in London for twelve months. James Miller suggested I come and join the little group of lodgers in his Victorian house in Baron's Court, near Hammersmith. That was fun, as we were all about the same age and got on up to a point. One of the others was Lucinda Airey, whose father, a retired general, had been GOC London District before becoming briefly the Private Secretary and Treasurer to the newly married Prince and Princess of Wales.

One gathered that was not an entirely rewarding appointment, though not as unhappy as Oliver Everett's time as the Princess of Wales's Private Secretary. Everett kindly suggested to the princess that she should read the biographies of Queen Alexandra and the brilliant volume on Queen Mary by James Pope-Hennessy, as a gentle way he thought of informing her about her future role. She had thrown the books to the ground and shouted, 'If you think I am going to read those ...' Such reported tantrums suggested there was a gulf between the increasingly mad reality and the sanctified public image of the princess which many *dévotes* still hold.

Nor is the popular legend true that Diana Spencer's marriage to Prince Charles had been arranged without her willing concurrence. In 1979 I was in Yorkshire with a party including Kenneth Rose (the journalist), as we planned to see the newly opened Beningborough Hall, near York, which had been restored by the National Trust as an outpost of the Portrait Gallery. There was also a group of young staying in the house, who were going to a dance for Alexandra Sitwell's twenty-first birthday at Renishaw. I found myself sitting at dinner next to an unknown eighteen year old blonde girl called Diana. She turned to me and opened the conversation, bang, with 'Who do you think the Prince of Wales is going to marry?' which shows she already had the prince on her mind well before her engagement in 1981. She had known the prince all her life, having been brought up at Park House in the grounds at Sandringham. (She hardly knew her irascible grandfather's house at Althorp.)

When I finally moved to my garage in the mews, in 1983, I could claim I had switched from a cellar to a stable. Instead of saying that I occupied the basement in the background of *Work*, the inevitable question from strangers was answered now: 'in the stable of Sidney Smith's horses'. The witty cleric and canon of St Paul's had lived at No. 14 Doughty Street. An old L.C.C. plaque there recorded his residence: 'Sidney Smith 1771-1845. Author and Wit. Lived Here.' I have toyed with the idea but never got round to acting on it, of erecting a blue plaque on my house saying: 'Sidney Smith's horses lived here'.

An old man who had lived in the mews before the war, when there were still horses not vans in the stables, told me that as children they used to jump out of the first floor windows for fun, on to the hay and straw piled on the roadway below. In 1983, the horses had long gone but there were three working garages still, and an electrical workshop and more commercial premises than houses. Now it is all quietish residential, flats and houses from end to end, though many of us work from home in the 'New Economy', but St George's Queen Square Church of England primary school (mainly Muslim children) to the south still fills the thoroughfare with cheerful zoo-like shrieks and noises at playtime.

Planning permission was necessary for the works. In response to a preliminary enquiry the council had assured that it would welcome the conversion of a garage to residential and that such a change would definitely not be a problem. When the formal application was submitted they said that they had had a 'change of policy' and were now promoting off-street parking as opposed to discouraging motors *per se*, and they wanted the garage retained. This was inconvenient as it left no space for such practical amenities as a kitchen. The fact that I do not drive and do not own a car was irrelevant. It is ironic that I who hate and disapprove of the internal combustion engine should be among the few souls in the world to have a compulsory garage forced upon them.

It was typical of public sector bureaucracy that it cannot implement the same policy for a few weeks, let alone hundreds of years like the great landed estates. Central London would be a much better place if local authority planning officers were abolished and the place run by the Crown Estate, the Grosvenors, Bedfords, the Howard de Waldens and their like, who have done a consistently good job of urban planning over a 300 year period, or so it seemed to me in the 1980s. With regard to the retained but unwanted garage forced on me by Camden Council (with all its green pretensions), I looked up the statutory minimum dimensions for a garage and reduced the area to that, which satisfied the officials but is too small for anything except a Mini. A hideous roller shutter was replaced with traditional boarded mews doors which disguised the skimpy dimensions behind. It left enough space to convert the remainder to living rooms with a kitchen and dining room divided by a Victorian glazed gothic screen; with three sash windows overlooking the neighbouring office garden at the back.

The gothic screen was a great find. I was walking along Curzon Street one day and as I passed the jewellers and silver shop on the corner of Shepherd Market opposite Heywood Hill's book shop, the contractors were stripping the interior, and a timber gothic screen with cusped tracery and a mirrored door was lying there. 'What are you doing with that?' I asked. 'Skipping it, mate,' was the answer. 'Please, can I have it?' They were amused and said yes; so I got my builder to go round with his truck to rescue it. It is the only feature of decorative interest in my little London house, though I also fitted other *objets trouvés* into the building. The simple panelled Georgian doors for instance came from a renovated house in Doughty Street. 'Not fire-proof, gov.' 'Could I buy them off you for my place in the mews?' 'If you give us ten bob we will bring them round now in a wheelbarrow.' The appropriately scaled Victorian cast iron fireplace in the sitting room also came from a building site.

Most of my architectural and history colleagues indulged in 'skipping'. One of them put it as his recreation in *Who's Who*. Andrew Edmunds, owner of the Georgian print shop, restaurant and the Academy Club in Lexington Street found a heap of eighteenth century shutters and panelling in a skip in Soho and used them to restore his own buildings. When we saw fixtures and fittings being illegally removed from listed buildings, we were able to get them reinstated. Thus, when Georgian woodwork was being torn out of a 1720s house in Dean Street, I got on to Westminster City Council whose 'enforcement officer' rushed round and had it all put back. The interior was then restored by Black's Club which still occupies the building. None of the members of that institution imagine that their convincing Georgian panelled rooms spent an afternoon lying on the pavement outside. Dan Cruickshank and I subsequently appeared as expert witnesses for the prosecution against the wicked developers who were convicted and fined, with costs. Illegal demolition of even part of listed buildings is a criminal offence.

Technically, all 'skipping' is illegal rather in the way that picking up a newly killed pheasant on the road is poaching, the contents of a skip count as private property. But the only person of my acquaintance who was ever apprehended by a bobby on the beat while rifling through an interesting looking builders' skip was the clergyman Anthony Symondson. 'What are you doing?' 'Oh, just looking for stained glass, officer,' turning round to reveal his dog collar. I must look proprietorial because I study the buildings when walking along a street. One night on the way home past a Georgian terrace in Bloomsbury where the glazing bars were being reinstated, the discarded Victorian plate glass sashes were on the pavement and a cockney was packing them into his van. He saw me and said 'Do you mind if I take these? For the cold frames on my allotment.' 'Not at all,' I replied truthfully, I hope not with too much of an air of carry on my good man.

The traditional appearance which I was able to give to the front of the Doughty Mews house gave me great pleasure. It is the only house in the street that *looks* unaltered from when first built by Mrs Doughty, a Dublin property developer in 1800. She owned a long narrow field adjoining the estates of the Foundling Hospital and Rugby School, and developed the area as Doughty Street with dependant mews to east and west. From her the property descended to the Tichbornes of Tichborne, Catholic baronets in Hampshire, best known for the Tichborne claimant, an Australian butcher who unsuccessfully claimed to be the heir, and the Tichborne Dole when bags of flour are blessed with incense and holy water by the priest in the portico of the house and distributed to the poor of the parish on the Feast of the Annunciation. I went once and it is quite a party on the front lawn. The property in Bloomsbury remained with the Doughty-Tichbornes until the 1930s when the freeholds were sold piecemeal, and my deeds begin with the Doughty-Tichborne ownership.

I replaced modern windows with double-hung three-pane Georgian sashes, touched up the brickwork with soot-wash to maintain the antique look, and painted all the external joinery Windsor Castle dark green using genuine lead paint acquired from the Crown Estate (prohibited for general use by the Common Market). The doors and windows and general design were copied from Westminster City Council's planning guide for mews conversions in reverse. I based my design on their picture showing a building 'before alteration'! This is one of many examples in my life of satisfyingly turning the clock backwards. In order to buy Doughty Mews, I sold all my shares which, on the principle that anything I use or like personally will not be profitable, were invested in chiming door bells, motels, second-hand cars (British Car Auctions) and condoms (the London Rubber Company). They did rather well, especially the cars and condoms, but Doughty Mews was the best investment I ever made and has been my ideal long-term London retreat.

Flookburgh, on the other hand, was neither ideal nor long-term. Though of considerable historic architectural interest, it was not Georgian and I wanted a Georgian house. It had low beamed ceilings and mullion windows. As the years passed, the drawbacks became more grating. The always slightly grim village started to be spoilt by 1980s 'home improvements' when Mrs Thatcher made everyone prosperous. Mild poverty is the best preservative. The trains deteriorated to an even more maddening extent, often missing the London connection in Lancaster. Road traffic increased in the village as people bought cars. The last straw was when the local authority which owned the adjoining field announced it was going to build an old peoples' home and commissioned a mediocre bungaloid design for the site overlooking my garden. I decided to look for a Georgian country house elsewhere in the north, not in an urgent way but with an eye open for when 'Castle Right' came along, in the way some people look for Mister or Miss Right. It did, and I fell for my ideal love, Beckside House, Barbon, on the same latitude as Flookburgh, but twenty miles inland in the

Front door of Beckside House. A design of James Gibbs, reproduced via Batty Langley by John Hird of Cartmel, a joiner turned architect.

foothills of the Pennines on the Lancashire-Westmorland border where the Lune valley becomes a noble Claudian landskip.

Flookburgh was sold on its 300th birthday, and my tenth anniversary there, in 1986, with mingled regrets and relief. There were aspects that I still miss, such as the sunnier, relatively frost-free, seaside climate which enabled me to grow a wider range of plants in the garden. I liked the grey, gritty 'ordinariness' of the village, and the delicious potted shrimps which one could buy from neighbours there but which do not travel inland. They become more expensive the further you are from Flookburgh, the centre of the shrimp world.

I bought Beckside unseen without even a photograph to guide me. I was going back to London one dreary Sunday evening in the early months of the year, and as the trains were running 'normally', that is unpunctually, the Furness link missed the London Express (as it was once optimistically known), stranding me in Lancaster with an hour to spare at the station with no tea room or warm waiting room. Nothing is more depressing than a British provincial town on a Sunday evening in winter when it is bleak, cold and wet with everything closed, even the pubs. Scotland, Wales and Northern Ireland are the worst, but England is not much better. I occupied myself by wandering around looking at the neglected Georgian buildings, tutting at poor alterations and the lack of intelligent care, and glancing at the windows of closed shops, especially those occupied by estate agents with their photographs of hideous bungalows and plasticated pebble-dashed villas with charabanc windows, for what seemed to me to be ridiculously inflated sums. Architectural quality is not something factored into English house prices.

Estate agents, their brochures, and their shop windows have long been a secret interest of mine. Agents use a particular distinctive language which is very revealing once you have mastered the code. Thus, a derelict nettle-infested wilderness is described as a 'landscape garden with huge potential'. Anything old-fashioned, rat-nibbled and inconvenient is called an 'attractive feature'. 'Open aspect towards the river', means there is a nuclear power station or industrial-scale pig farm on the far bank. 'A property with scope for development and improvement' means currently derelict and uninhabitable. 'Tastefully modernised' means with plastic avocado bath or 'on sweet' shower fitted into a tiny cupboard. Armed with my Bletchley-code-crib to house-agents speak, I was knocked over backwards, as if by a hammer in the middle of my forehead, to see in the corner of an obscure, now-defunct, house-agents' window an *unillustrated* advertisement for my dream dwelling.

It read: 'A listed 8 bedroom Georgian house in Need of Renovation Quietly Situated in *c*2 Acres of Grounds with River Frontage on the Very Fringe of the Delightful and Much Sought After Lunesdale Village of Barbon.' I could barely contain myself. What could I do? The shop was closed. I made a note of the details and the agent's telephone number, and caught the train to London in a state of uncontrollable excitement. People sitting near me in the carriage gave me funny looks, as they thought I must be high on drugs. What if the object of desire had already gone? The dusty advertisement could be out of date. Was it possible to be gazumped on Sunday night in March in Lancaster?

I barely slept that night and the following morning at 9 o'clock prompt, I rang the agents. The telephone was answered without urgency by a youngish voice. I tried to hide my nervousness and enthusiasm. 'That old house in Barbon, what is wrong with it? Is the roof about to collapse?' to my amazement the young man at the other end of the line said, 'Oh no, structurally it is not in bad shape, the roof should last another twenty years when it will eventually need re-slating ... but, it needs a lot doing inside, you should see *the* bath, cast iron on paw feet, with a funny plunger plug; that will have to be replaced...' Untouched Georgian, *and* a Victorian cast iron bath! Could such a thing exist in 1986? I continued, 'Any interest...?' More guardedly, 'Yes, we have someone *very* keen who wants to turn it into a bed-and-breakfast business, the perfect solution for a place like that. About to put in an offer.' I felt as if my desired was about to be raped. Bed and Breakfast!

That would mean plastic 'on sweets' in every room. 'I will buy it,' I said. Agent, rather startled, 'When would you like to visit and inspect? Shall I make an appointment for you, and will you want a surveyor's report done?' 'No,' I replied, 'can I exchange contracts now, my solicitors and bank are...', and so Beckside House was bought, unseen, on the telephone on a Monday morning before going into the Historic Buildings office for an ordinary day's work.

I did visit on a gloomy wet day before completing the purchase. It is always a good idea to visit a property when it is raining, then you can see the leaks. I could hardly believe my eyes. The place was superficially derelict, the garden an overgrown jungle, some of the Crown Glass window panes cracked, the outbuildings ruinous. The last occupant, a Mrs Maxwell, had died exactly six years previously in April 1980, and the place had been empty since. There had been an outbreak of dry rot but that had been dealt with, and the house came with a thirty year Rentokil guarantee. Structural minutiae were, however, beside the point. It was the magic phrase 'in need of renovation' that had convinced me to buy in the first place.

Had the particulars said 'tastefully modernised', I would have run a mile. Not only was the interior untouched; but apart from some minor works *circa* 1890, nothing had been touched since the house was built in 1767. It was miraculously unaltered and intact. The joinery and fittings were exceptional, a mad or drunk carpenter's fantasy inspired by the pattern books of Batty Langley: *The Builders Jewel* of 1741 and similar eighteenth century publications. Every room had a carved chimney-piece with lugged architraves. The staircase had three turned wood balusters to each step and gristly carved rococo tread ends. There were cornices and dadoes, panelled doors, and gothick details, especially in the hall and dining room (Eating Room) which was complete with an inbuilt pedimented buffet or china cupboard, the doors still glazed with authentic Crown Glass panes. Every H or L wrought iron hinge, every brass lock escutcheon survived.

Beckside House was Batty Langley's 'Design for a Small House'

Beckside House, Barbon. Bought unseen by JMR in 1986 as "listed Georgian House in need of renovation".

carried into effect. Because of the pattern-book influence, several of the fittings had very grand architectural derivations: the pedimented stone doorcase at the front came from James Gibbs's *Book of Architecture* (1728). The chimney-piece in the Common Parlour, my drawing room, was a design of Inigo Jones. Yet, everything was made even more charming by provincial amateur touches. Although the proportions were perfect and thanks to Batty Langley based on the Golden Section, nothing was quite symmetrical or centred. Vernacular and idiosyncratic details had crept into the classical carving. The egg and dart mouldings had more than a touch of turnip and dart. By London standards the building was spectacularly old-fashioned, more than thirty or forty years out of date when it was built. While the staircase or the raised and fielded panels were identical to those in houses in Soho, Covent

Garden or Mayfair, they had been created in the 1720s and 1730s, whereas Beckside was dated 1767 on the upstairs central window lintel. In architectural terms it was far more than I was expecting. Fortune favours the brave. Hugh Massingberd called my punt 'the fluke of Flookburgh'. Neither the dull damp weather, nor the air of dereliction could detract from my euphoria.

When leaving, I encountered a further stroke of good luck. The cottage across the stone bridge on the other side of the beck, just outside the front gate, had a painted sign which read 'J. Nelson & Sons. Builders. Established 1906'. I noted the telephone and later rang Mr Nelson. He was called Peter and seemed a bit non-committal but I explained that I had bought Beckside and it needed a lot of repair work; would he be interested in the job. It turned out that not only was he the local builder, but that his family had looked after Beckside for three generations and he knew it in its strengths and weaknesses like a hospital patient. His grandfather had re-roofed the house nearly one hundred years earlier. Peter Nelson's own first job on leaving school at fourteen had been the external render on the west gable wall. My architect keeps saying I should take it off as it is cement and I should re-point with lime mortar but I keep the 1960s render as it is not unsightly, does no harm, and is a memento of Peter's former care of the house, which is now part of the history of the building. Another memento is the tree he gave me in the garden. When one points out the Nelson Oak, now forty feet high, visitors say where is Wellington?

Peter Nelson knew all sorts of essential details which otherwise it would have taken years to discover, such as the place in the lane outside the front gate where was buried the stop cock for the mains water supply. The water at Barbon comes from Thirlmere in the Lake District. It is very soft compared to London, and I always wash my hair in the country as there is none of the soapy scum of London. That sounds a rather Edwardian remark like having one's own Jersey milk brought up specially on the morning train, but is just practical. The kettles do not scale up either in the country.

The initial building contract began in June 1986 and continued until the end of the year, and work has been almost continuous ever since. In those years I acted as my own architect with Peter, and he assembled the team of craftsmen to restore the Georgian windows, install plumbing, and other work, though I used Robert Boak, the electrician from Flookburgh, who had worked for me at the Manor House there to re-wire. Flookburgh was a useful trial run for the bigger restoration project on which I now embarked. Robert was a great Viking of a man, and used to sing while he was working. You could tell whether things were going smoothly or not by the register of the song; strong, dark, bass sounds meant he was having difficulty pulling the wires through a tight space beneath a thick joist.

We put in two or three new bathrooms (but kept the cast iron beauty), a kitchen, oil-fired heating, new drains, new water pipes and all that sort of thing, as well as gently nursing the Georgian architecture back to life. I won't bore you with the details, as tales of other people's building work are on a par with 'our holiday snaps' or those show-off round-robin Christmas letters bragging about Oscar and Henrietta's gap year in Bali, or the brilliant concert just organised for a very worthy Kiddees Charity ... I will just say that all my building work at Barbon in the 1980s and 1990s gave me great satisfaction, and I enjoyed working on the resuscitation of the house with a succession of skilled, talented, interested craftsmen, very unlike pre-Polish-builders in London.

I feel almost superstitious about my luck at Barbon. Discovering and acquiring the house in the first place, and then the fulfilling job of restoring the building and creating the garden seem altogether too good to be true. Was it the working of Divine Providence? What does it entail? I cannot possibly deserve it. Does God have some terrible nemesis in prospect to even the score? It is not fair. But it does give me an urge to repay my worldly debt, as far as I can. I do *try* to be kind to widows and orphans. Beckside, of which I consider myself to be the curator, has given a strong central theme to my life for the last thirty-five years.

Over time I have pieced together the story of the house; why it was built, who has lived there, the reasons for the miraculous, unaltered survival. I bought it from Joseph Gibson out of his Settled Estate. His predecessor, also Joseph Gibson, had acquired it in 1856, but it had never been the Gibson's main house as they had a bigger Tudorbethan seat designed by Webster of Kendal in 1834, Whelprigg, to the south of the village. During their ownership, Beckside had been lived in by spinster aunts such as Miss Gibson who had died in 1926, or had been let to tenants. It had been kept in reasonable structural repair, but never altered or 'improved'.

Though the house and surrounding land had belonged to the Gibsons for over a hundred years, they had not built it in the first place. The initials on the 1767 dated lintel were G^{T}A. When I researched them, I discovered they stood for George and Anne Turner. The Turners were another Barbon family formerly copyhold tenants who, like the Gibsons, Garnets, and Hardys, had accumulated land and risen to gentry status in the eighteenth century, after the enfranchisement of the manor in 1716 by Richard Shuttleworth of Gawthorpe whose ancestor Sir Richard Shuttleworth had bought it in the reign of Elizabeth I and whose descendant Lord Shuttleworth still owns the manor and the surrounding 7,000 acres, including the medieval park and enclosing fells.

Turners built up their property, enclosed and improved it, and by the mid-eighteenth century owned several farms: Yew Tree, Eskholme, and Beckgate, as well as Beckside, and property in Kirkby Lonsdale and other surrounding parishes. These had all been sold over the years and by 1986 only the house and garden remained. George Turner built the new house out of his agricultural prosperity. George and Anne had no children but occupied the house with his aged mother who lived to be ninety, and the house was designed with two principal bedrooms and dressing rooms, and a three-seater privy in the garden. Incidentally, the etiquette of Georgian multi-seat privies was not that you all sat there together, holding hands, as in the popular imagination, but that you had your own personal bespoke seat for when you did visit.

The present house is dated 1767, but there was an older house on the site which was recorded in the ownership of Thomas Garnet of 'Beckside in Barbon' in 1690. It is possible that the lower west wing (later washhouse, dairy, stable and manservants' bothy) was the 17th century predecessor house retained as domestic offices when the new house was erected to the east. The Garnets were among a small group of established statesmen or copyholders at Barbon in the 16th and 17th centuries.

Certain biographical details can be gleaned about George Turner: he died aged 57 in January 1782 (Kirkby Lonsdale Parish Register), but his mother lived to be 90, a remarkable achievement in the 18th century. They are buried in a stone table tomb adjoining the south porch of Kirkby Lonsdale churchyard. (Restored with a grant from the Georgian Group in 2008). George Turner and his family were friends of Thomas Fenwick, lawyer and landowner, of Burrow Hall, Lancashire (inherited from his mother) whose diaries were edited by Jennifer Holt for the List And Index Society in four volumes in 2012. Fenwick records riding from Burrow to Barbon to drink wine with George Turner and their dining together in Kirkby Lonsdale on roast chicken, leg of mutton, pickled sea trout, cold beef, peas and potatoes; George Turner (as a Freehold landowner) voted for Fenwick in the contested 1768 Westmorland Election, in which Fenwick won the Kendal Division Seat against the Lowther Tory candidate.

George Turner built Beckside in 1767 when he was 42 years old which is interesting as he and his wife Anne had no children and therefore no immediate descendants. After the Turners, the house belonged in the early-19th century to the Walker family, until it was purchased from them on 9 December 1856 by the Gibsons of Whelprigg for £6,300. The Gibsons were landed gentry, owning over 3,000 acres and most of the village of Barbon, and serving as High Sheriff and JPs in the 19th century. It belonged to the Gibsons as part of their larger property-holding at Barbon, for over 100 years until bought by the present owner from Joseph Hollins Gibson in April 1986.

Until the Victorian vicarage was built for the first vicar of Barbon, the Revd James Harrison, in 1870, Beckside was for a time occupied by the curate. (Historically Barbon was a chapel of ease within the parish of Kirkby Lonsdale). From the late-19th century until her death in 1926, the house was occupied by Miss Gibson, the aunt of the squire, who carried out some minor improvements *c*1900. After her death it was let (for 10s a week) from 1926 to John Davis, the local land-agent and his wife Nellie, a keen gardener, until they moved away in 1966 after his retirement. The local land agents firm Davis & Bowring was founded and run from Beckside until it moved into Kirkby Lonsdale during the Second World War because of petrol rationing. The Davises were the last people to live in the whole house. It was let out in the late 1960s and 1970s to eccentric tenants who occupied odd rooms, and then lay empty. As far as is known, no children have ever been born or lived in the house.

This story of unusual ownership explains the remarkable survival of the Georgian interior in an unaltered state. After purchase by the Gibsons in 1856, no structural alterations were made, though the fabric was maintained in good repair by the estate builders. Thus many of the sash windows at the front retain original Crown glass, and the outbuildings include an intact 3-seater privy and a simple Georgian beebole, and even the garden retains its Georgian layout with a formal lawn in front of the house and a 'shrubbery' or 'wilderness' to the side with old yews, Scots pines, beech and Portuguese laurels, and winding grass paths.

The design and construction of the house is not documented, but certain stylistic peculiarities point to the hand of John Hird of Cartmel as the designer/builder. Hird was active in north Lancashire and Westmorland in the 1760s and 1770s, designing houses in Lancaster and Kendal, the Assembly Room at the Bull and Royal in Preston, Leighton Hall in 1765, the part gothicisation of Sizergh Castle, the nave of Preston parish church in 1770 and the chapel at Flookburgh in 1777 (both replaced in the 19th century). He also remodelled Witherslack church in 1767 and the occurrence there of certain idiosyncratic details, especially a St Andrew's cross with leaves at the interstices is paralleled at Beckside and can be treated almost as Hird's signature motif.

Hird was a carpenter from Kirkleatham in North Yorkshire who came as part of Carr of York's team of craftsmen to work on Holker Hall, Cark-in-Cartmel, for the Cavendishes. He stayed and married a farmer's daughter from Cartmel. In 1763 when he became a Freeman of Preston, he was described as a 'house carpenter of Kendal'.

The design executed by Hird, from Langley's engravings, for the Turners is an endearing mix of sophistication and naivety. All the woodwork and carving is nevertheless of good technical quality, and points to Hird's training as a carpenter. Most of the important features like the chimney-pieces, the china cupboard in the Eating Room, the archway in the hall, the staircase are all of carved wood. Apart from moulded classical cornices in the principal rooms, hall and staircase, there is no plasterwork. All the 18th century chimney-pieces are of carved wood except the 'Inigo Jones' one in the Parlour which alone is of stone. This prominence given to carpentry reinforces the attribution to John Hird as 'architect'/builder.

Barbon has been the centre of my life for thirty-five years. I spend half the year there, with a couple of months in December-January, and again in August-September, and an increasingly long period at Easter and Spring when the weather, garden and landscape are at their best. Otherwise I go there for alternate 'weekends' from Thursday to Tuesday in 'term-time'. Friends, family, godchildren, come and stay all the time. When I told my neighbour Henry Bowring at Whelprigg (whose grandfather bought that house from the Gibsons in 1920) that I have an average of a hundred guests to stay a year, he said 'Oh, I have two hundred', but Henry is professionally social, has around thirty godchildren, and Whelprigg is a bigger house, thirteen extra bedrooms having been added in 1913. I only have eight bedrooms and four bathrooms (*No* 'on sweets'). Over the years visitors have left tributes, including drawings, and photographs by successive *Country Life* photographers while staying to take pictures for articles on northern houses. Thus I have good photographs of the front of the house by both Mark Fiennes and Paul Barker, both alas now dead. Michael Gillingham, 'Spinkery Sparkery' of Fournier Street in Spitalfields, also now dead, wrote a Thompsonian ode in the garden on his first visit in August 1988. It captures the revived spirit of Beckside in elegant neo-Augustan rhymes:

An Ode to his friend Dr Robinſon
upon a viſit to Barbon Hall

Dear Barbon Beck! I hear thy murmur sweet
As I recline upon this graſſy Seat,
Becalm'd and traceried o'er with Hoary Art
To nurſe the Gothick fire within my Heart:
Yet ſtill I trace the Shades of Greece and Rome
Within the Walls of this, mine Auncient Home:
Embracing thus all art of Olden Time
In Architecture, and the Muſe's Rhyme.

by Mr M. G. to his friend
Dr JMR
ye 13 Auguſt MCMLXXXVIII

7

The New Georgians

I JOINED THE Society for the Protection of Ancient Buildings (SPAB) as a schoolboy, and later the Georgian Group and the Victorian Society (Vixoc) while at university. I was present at the founding of SAVE Britain's Heritage, the most effective historic buildings campaigner, in 1975. It has been fulfilling to support these admirable preservation societies over a life-time. An Easter holiday was once spent helping an enthusiastic volunteer restore the windmill at Framsden in Suffolk for SPAB. For the Vixoc, there was involvement in the transformation of Linley Sambourne's House in Stafford Terrace, Kensington, from the London home of Sambourne's grand-daughter, the Countess of Rosse, to a public museum. The Victorian Society had been founded in the drawing room there in 1958. Hermione Hobhouse, Secretary of the Vixoc and I took it in turns to stay in the house during the inter-regnum, having a daily bottle of milk delivered to the front door step, to keep up the illusion of the place being lived in. One had to wash in the Victorian marble bath off the upper half landing. The secret with a marble bath is to run the hot water in first and let the marble warm up for a time before you sit in it, otherwise marble baths can be very uncomfortable and they may not need any cold water added.

Flora Pilkington helped compile an inventory of the contents, for Lady Rosse and her old housekeeper before they left Stafford Terrace. Anne Rosse was wonderfully snobbish and you could calculate the exact rank of the person she was talking to by the amount of gush. If she said, 'You absolutely wonderful, darling person, how tremendously splendid and kind,' it meant you were a servant. If she said, 'Thank you. That's fine,' it meant you were above the salt. While we were sorting the things, she gave me a Victorian morning coat which had been made for her uncle Roy Sambourne in around 1890. Holding it up while clearing out a cupboard, she said, 'This will fit you, would you like it?' I still wear it though it is now more sage green with age rather than black. At least it doesn't look like Moss Bros. It often attracts comment from the policeman on the gate checking identity and invitations at the Garden Party. One of the perks of being an Officer of Arms is that we are invited every year, though we do not do anything there, unlike the Gentleman of Arms who present selected guests to the Queen as she makes her way slowly across the Lawn from the palace to the Royal Tea Tent. It also gains attention at weddings. When people comment, 'A green coat—how unusual,' The reply is, 'Yes, it is over a hundred years old and was made for Lord Snowdon's great-uncle.'

Of all the Amenity Societies, the Georgian Group has been the most time-consuming. Elected a trustee on the Executive Committee in February 1981, I served for over thirty years, until February 2014. I became Vice Chairman in 1990, and as is often the case in such roles, 'the vice' did much of the work and gave direction alongside a succession of chairmen, from Jeremy Benson, an architect and effective campaigner, to Diane Nutting. My initiatives as Vice Chairman included founding the Young Georgians for those under the age of thirty, to attract twenty-year-olds and try to bring down the average age of the members who tended to be on the 'mature' side; and, as one trustee said, were dominated by 'the Kensington Widows', a splendid breed who have alas almost died out. The first chairman of the Young Georgians in 1990 was Orlando Rock, now chairman of Christies UK. He was just starting to work in the company thirty years ago. The trouble with the Young Georgians is that they grew into old Georgians, involving a continuous search for new fledglings. Orlando is also now, with his wife Miranda, joint custodian of Burghley House in the Soke of Peterborough, where I later sat on the Preservation Trust for five years.

Another policy at the Georgian Group that we pursued was the employment of proper case workers and the establishment of a case-work sub-committee to deal with the principal charitable work of the group, the preservation of eighteenth century buildings. Before that, everything was done by the Secretary Eleanor Murray, with one assistant. The aim was to have case-workers for different areas including Wales, and to employ bright young people, straight from university. We could not afford grown-up salaries and the best policy was to have clever short-term enthusiasts for two or three years on the low wages the charity could afford, rather than longer-serving, less effective, mediocrities. Many of the Georgian case workers moved on to organisations like English Heritage, becoming historic buildings inspectors after their start with us, but they provided a useful network of contacts after they moved on. We used to joke that we should charge English Heritage for training staff for them. One of the points of the new Casework Committee, which I chaired, was to monitor and assist the case-workers, to achieve a high quality and informed consistency of response. The committee also brought in outside expertise, architects, structural engineers and curators, to lend professional clout to the Group's approach to building conservation, and help ameliorate suspicions that the Group existed chiefly to visit ducal rose gardens.

Following the example of the Vixoc we also set up regional groups in South Yorkshire, Lancashire, Essex and East Anglia, and Gloucestershire and the West, to complement the existing East Yorkshire Georgian Society and the Bath Preservation Trust. These sub-groups flourished for a time, but gradually faded out after the 1990s for a variety of reasons, but mainly the death or retirement of the driving force local member, and later a lack of support from head office. The Georgian Group never developed a federal character, and has become increasingly centralised over the years. In the 1980s there had been serious thought of amalgamating with SPAB, a richer, older preservation charity, founded by William Morris in 1877. The architect Jeremy Benson was at the time chairman of both organisations. He was an amusing man in the chair, as he never drew breath, and then told all the rest of us we were talking too much. He brought brown envelopes of seeds from his garden at Walpole House, Chiswick Mall, and offered them around. The hellebores and aquilegia at Beckside were grown from Jeremy's seeds.

The Group had begun as part of SPAB in 1937, which is why it is called the Georgian Group, not the Georgian Society, because it was the new subsidiary *group* of the older Ancient Buildings Society and was formed to protect and restore eighteenth century buildings at a time when official policy, which SPAB followed, considered anything after 1715 to be 'modern' and not worth bothering about. My favourite example of that blinkered approach was the old Royal Commission on Historical Monuments report on Wentworth Woodhouse in Yorkshire which devoted a paragraph to the exiguous remains of a Roman road in the park and added 'the mansion is modern'. Full stop. The Georgian Group soon became independent but kept its original appellation and has done so, but not without conscious retro effort in the 1980s and 1990s when clueless 'management consultants' held sway and tried to change the name to Society to be 'tidy'.

SPAB was in the process of moving to a silk weaver's house at 37 Spital Square in Spitalfields which was being restored for them by Julian Harrap. The Jeremy Benson amalgamation campaign persuaded the Georgian Group trustees to move from their small grace and favour office on the Grosvenor Estate at 2 Chester Street, Belgravia, which passed to the new Historic Houses Association, and into the building in Spital Square with SPAB. The Georgian's chairman, who succeeded Jeremy, Bill Harris, a QC, went along with it. The argument was that it made sense to share facilities, which the accountants and business consultants advised would reduce the Group's costs. A panelled office in a restored early-Georgian house seemed an appropriate location. The economic argument, however, proved false. SPAB charged £30,000 a year rent for the top floor when it was occupied by the Georgians. It turned out that we still needed all our own office equipment like copying and fax machines and telephone lines, so the move not only failed to reduce costs but increased them by lumbering the Group with a serious commercial rent without any obvious benefits from sharing a building.

There is moreover a strong philosophical and policy argument for remaining independent. The Group had broken away from SPAB in 1937 because it did not share the strict William Morris principles of the Society. Morris and his disciples objected to 'restoration' as opposed to 'protection' of old buildings. With ancient structures like crook cottages and vernacular barns, such an approach made sense, as the antiquity of the fabric was part of the historic interest, but was much less so with a Georgian building where the artistic concept, the proportions, the symmetry, the architect's original design recorded in drawings, were more important.

The Georgian Group believes in scholarly restoration. It supported the full reinstatement of fire damaged interiors at Uppark and Windsor Castle to their original form after the fires in the 1990s. SPAB did not. It advocated that the destroyed staircase at Uppark should be replaced not in replica but in stainless steel, or that modern rooms using modern materials should be installed at Windsor, despite the survival of the integral George IV contents. The scholarly restoration of Christ Church, Spitalfields to Hawksmoor's scrupulously researched original design, reinstating his two tier side windows and the galleries, was an example of the 'Georgian Approach', as was the recreation of the gutted interior of St John Smith Square after the war by Marshall Sisson to Thomas Archer's design, rather than back in the altered form in which it existed before the blitz. Architect members of the Georgian Group in the 1950s—Albert Richardson and Claud Phillimore, as well as Sisson, had advocated and carried out careful restorations partly in replica of bomb damaged London churches, the Bath Assembly Rooms, or the derelict Lord Burlington's Chiswick Villa, removing later additions. The Georgian Group believes in recreating missing architectural features where there is scholarly evidence, and making aesthetically informed decisions governed by the overall impact of the artistic design and original concept. SPAB opposes such an approach. It advocates that any new work or repair should be radically different to indicate clearly what is original and what is new. SPAB prefers patchwork to the Georgian Group's seamless aesthetic unity.

These views represent two different philosophies of conservation. Good arguments can be made for both approaches, and I will not get bogged down in an esoteric debate here. The point is that with two divergent philosophical and aesthetic approaches, it was more sensible for the Georgian Group to maintain its independence. The younger members of the committee thought so in the 1980s and early 1990s. They advocated the acquisition by the Group of its own Georgian building to serve as headquarters, office, a place for education and lectures, possibly a source of income, and an exemplar of the correct restoration of a Georgian house. Neil Burton, who succeeded Roger White as secretary at that time, was a strong advocate of independent premises, as was Giles Waterfield, Giles Worsley, Susan Anstruther, and Sophie Andreae among the trustees; as of course was I.

Various premises were considered. There was a possibility that the philanthropist, Simon Sainsbury, a generous supporter of historic buildings and a member of the Group, might help fund the acquisition of a house for us. Glyn Boyd Harte, then in economic difficulties thanks to Inland Revenue demands, offered to sell his house in Percy Street, Fitzrovia, to the Group, but Colin Amery, architectural advisor to Sainsburys, and a member of the Georgian Group Council (a sort of limbo to which were 'promoted' those trustees who wished to retire or were unable to attend committee meetings) advised Simon Sainsbury not to fund such an acquisition. The upshot was that Simon changed his mind and decided not to contribute to the Georgian premises fund. A cheaper early-nineteenth century house in Kennington was available and was in reasonable condition. It seemed to meet the criteria, but the Georgian's staff, who hated Spitalfields, let it be known that they did not wish to work outside the Circle Line. So that was that. It

Colin Amery: detail from a portrait by Dorothy Girouard

narrowed the field to a Georgian house within the Circle Line. There were a lot of them but most were too expensive.

Just when acquiring a property seemed to be impossible, the Group was alerted to the closure of a small branch bank in Fitzroy Square. It was not far from Glyn's house which had become lodged in the trustees' minds as a perfect house in a perfect location. The redundant bank building was even more perfect. It was in the best terrace on the east side of Fitzroy Square, a Grade I town house designed by Robert Adam. The bank was off-loading in the early 1990s, the beginning of the corporate programme to close every branch bank in the country. After all what are banks for? To serve customers at their convenience, or to provide golden handshakes and pensions for their own staff? Fred Goodwin provided the answer to that a few years later. This negative approach came to mind when a future secretary of the Georgian Group, Bruno (Robert) Bargery said to me: 'Running the Group would be fine if it did not have any members.' To my surprise, he meant it.

The bank was getting rid of 'redundant plant', and being a bank was not that concerned about money. Therefore it was prepared to let us have the building for a knockdown £450,000. Even in 1994, that was a 'fair' price for a large, four-storeyed Portland Stone-fronted, Adam house in a prime London square. It is worth at least several million today. Even at that ridiculously low purchase price, some of the less-imaginative and less financially astute trustees showed signs of foot-dragging. I wish now I had bought it for myself, and not bothered to convince the Georgian Group to take the plunge. As things developed in the longer term, I am not sure they were worthy of it. To be fair to the bank, it realised it was letting us have a bargain, and said 'you are a charity, you must think of it as our contribution to your charitable work'.

By 1994, we had the money to buy our house and our freedom, and to escape from SPAB. This was thanks to the generosity of a deceased member, Sir Philip Shelburne. He was a bachelor member, a banker with a Georgian house in Salisbury Cathedral Close. The Group had visited on one of the activities organised for members and they had so charmed Sir Philip with their good manners and knowledgeable appreciation of his house and things, that he added a codicil to his will. When he died a couple of years later, it turned out that he had left his residuary estate half and half to the donkey sanctuary in Alexandria and to the Georgian Group. His residuary estate included his furniture, and Christies were able to sell it so well, that in the end the Georgian Group received around a million pounds, which enabled it to buy 6 Fitzroy Square from the NatWest and to restore it and convert the top floor into two flats to let out and bring in rental income. It transformed the financial situation of the Group, as the flats were let by a good independent outside agent for £15,000 a year each. Thus, Fitzroy Square immediately made the Group £60,000 a year better off, with a saving of £30,000 on the rent of Spital Square, and the plus of £30,000 income from the Fitzroy Square rents. We are very grateful to Sir Philip. I hope the Egyptian donkeys are too. His portrait which he also left us hangs in the library at Fitzroy Square.

Neil Burton, Susan Anstruther, Giles Worsley and I together oversaw the restoration and conversion. Susan was the wife of Sir Ian Anstruther, historian of the Eglinton Tournament, and owner of the Thurlow Estate (opposite Brompton Oratory) in London, and the 3,000 acre Barlavington estate in Sussex. She was an architect, with practical experience of managing urban property, and professional skills. Susan played a key role in the Fitzroy Square project, introducing a firm of builders who worked with her regularly in South Kensington, though some of us thought that a band of Poles might have been more efficient. It was slightly awkward for the job architect, having a professional member of the committee as his client giving directions, and builders not of his choosing. Neil, with his hard work and energy, kept the team together and was able to conclude the work on site successfully. Nevertheless it was a huge advantage to the Georgian Group, embarking as a novice on large-scale building work, to have someone of Susan's experience on the Fitzroy Square House sub-committee.

We appointed as architect James Gorst, a pupil of John Outram, who had done Giles Worsley's London house and also worked for me in London, so we could vouch for him. Neil acted almost as clerk of works. The main job was the ground floor which had been knocked through and stripped out to create a single banking hall. We put all the dividing walls back, between the entrance hall and the front and back rooms. The first floor was subdivided into little offices by plasterboard partitions, but they came out easily enough, restoring the rooms on the *piano nobile* to their spacious Adam proportions. The only insoluble problem was a huge concrete and steel strong room, a giant safe, in the middle of the basement which proved impossible to remove without demolishing the building. It is still there, but makes a good place to store the Nescafe for the office elevenses.

Patrick Baty of Papers and Paints did 'scrapes', I mean 'paint analysis', to ascertain the original colours for the rooms, which he mixed and provided: pink on the ground floor, green on the first floor, stone-colour in the hall and staircase, just as you would have imagined. Chesneys and Jamb reproduced the missing marble chimney-pieces in the principal rooms from the evidence of old photographs. The ground floor ones had been removed when making the banking hall, and the two on the first floor 'disappeared' during the inter-regnum. The American friends of the Georgian Group who had been established by Bill Harris, paid for glazed mahogany Georgian bookcases for the library on the ground floor. I was walking down Tower Bridge Road from the City towards Bermondsey Market for its dawn Friday sale of 'antiques' and stolen goods and noticed a workshop on the left 'restoring' the said antiques. I went in and asked whether they could provide some bookcases. 'How many', they said. Oh, about four should be enough, different sizes to fit three walls of a room and flank a fireplace. 'Fine', they said, 'we will deliver them next week.' So we have a matching set of well-proportioned 'antique' glazed mahogany bookcases, from Bermondsey, 1995 vintage.

The acquisition and restoration of No. 6 Fitzroy Square in 1994-1995 was the highpoint of the Georgian Group's revival in the 1980s and 1990s, years which were among the charity's glory days. 1987 was the fiftieth anniversary of the Group and was celebrated in a fitting manner. The royal patron, Queen Elizabeth, presided over the fiftieth birthday party with her corgis in the state rooms at St James Palace, having stepped through a gib door from Clarence House to greet the members in the Throne Room.

A couple of years earlier in 1985, the younger trustees forming an Activities Committee, had organised a splendid Georgian Rout in anticipation, in the William Chambers Fine Rooms at Somerset House, then empty prior to restoration by the Courtauld Institute. The Rout was intended to demonstrate the rejuvenated character of the Group, and was inspired by the pre-War Georgian Ball and *fête champêtre* given to raise money for the fledgling Group, by

Programme cover for the Georgian Rout at Somerset House 1985.

'Grandy' Jersey and his American film star wife Virginia Cherrill in July 1939 at Osterley Park. The 1939 ball at Osterley was described by American *Life* magazine as the 'most spectacular charity party of a spectacular London social season'. The guests included Cecil Beaton, Diana Cooper, Peter Glenville (son of the actress Dorothy Ward) and Douglas Fairbanks. The entertainments included Cumberland Wrestling, an orchestra on a raft in the lake playing Handel, and fireworks. The barmaids and footmen, and most of the guests, wore Georgian costume. The barmaids were especially convincing, and the footmen wore powdered wigs. Lord Antrim dressed as a cardinal. Lord Jersey wore a suit copied from the Allan Ramsey portrait of his ancestor the banker Sir Francis Child, while his wife's dress was designed by Oliver Messel, to complement her diamond tiara. We aimed in 1985 to outdo the Osterley party, and succeeded.

The Fine Rooms at Somerset House were the ideal setting, an enfilade of magnificent neo-classical spaces with stucco ceilings, incorporating paintings by Benjamin West, Biaggio Rebecca and Angelica Kauffman, and marble chimney-pieces. We had got wind through Robin Wyatt, a Wyatt descendant in the Ministry of Works, that we might be able to use them following the removal of the General Register of Births, Deaths and Marriages and before the Courtauld took them over. The fact that they were empty and not yet restored gave us a free hand and meant we did not need to be too precious. The only problem was the theatrical semi-circular stone cantilevered West Staircase, the 'starecase' of Rowlandson's cartoon showing female visitors to the Royal Academy Summer Exhibition falling down with their skirts round their heads. The Ministry of Works insisted on propping the stairs with scaffold poles, though it probably was not necessary. The poles were disguised successfully with floral decoration, and bare-chested youths in silver loin cloths scattering silver stars into the well took the eyes of arriving guests away from the utilitarian underpinning. The rooms were transformed for the occasion by Paul Dyson, an active member of the group (now director of communication at the Goldsmiths Company). Paul was then the window dresser at Harvey Nicks and a jewellery designer. He produced a series of tall papier-mâché campanula urns painted to look like lapis lazuli, worthy of the Winter Palace, and filled them with huge flower arrangements. The flowers for the evening were the work of Countess Badeni, English wife of a Polish/Austrian noble, and Maria Perry-Robinson, actress and florist, of Distinctive Flowers. The flowers were as spectacular as Paul's designs for the decoration. The West Ante-Room was used for taking photographs of the participants, the former Royal Society Meeting Room was the ballroom for dancing Minuets, the East Ante-Room a studio for silhouettes which proved very popular, the old Society of Antiquaries Meeting Room became the Card Room with gaming organised by the Clermont Club, the smartest West End gambling den. The Royal Academy Council room was for Sitting Out and the Royal Academy Antiques Room was the Eating Room with refreshments: puddings and champagne. The champagne was organised from the Travellers Club. The security and maintenance staff at Somerset House helped themselves to a case, but they probably deserved it as we had given them a lot of extra work.

Entertainments included dancing Minuets, organised by the Covent Garden Dance Company who conducted rehearsals between the dances to ensure participants could master the intricate steps. Music was provided by Augustine Ford and the Kew Band. His father, Brinsley, dressed as the Grand Master of the Society of Dilettanti (which he was), presided with aplomb over the auction of drawings and pictures and small Georgian antiques presented by dealers and artists, Mallets, Michael Gillingham, Anthony Mould, Hugh Casson and John Piper, and wine from Berry Bros. There was also a raffle, the prizes for which and the gaming prizes were also presented by supporters, as well as the usual books from members like Lord Anglesey, John Julius Norwich, Marcus Binney, David Watkin, and Ben Weinreb, they included a haircut at Trumpers, and a day's hunting with the Pytchley & Quorn. Alan Powers staged two performances of a Georgian Punch and Judy

Alan and Susanna Powers and Glynn and Carrie Boyd Harte with matching white Renaults. They helped with the Georgian Rout at Somerset House in 1987.
Alan designed and produced a puppet theatre with Sir John and Lady Vanbrugh. Glynn gave some of the guests food poisoning by serving authentic Georgian food at a dinner party beforehand.

Show, starring Vanbrugh in a model theatre, and his wife, all of which he wrote and designed himself. The silhouettes, skilfully cut in quick sittings by David Gilbert and Robin Whiteside of the 'World of Silhouettes', sold like hot cakes.

The photographer (provided by *Harpers & Queen*) was kept busy all evening, too, as people were keen to be recorded in their eighteenth century finery. Some of the pictures were published in the write-ups in magazines. We were especially fortunate to be able to draw on the wardrobe of English National Opera, thanks to Nick John and Henrietta Bredin, which provided authentic Georgian outfits. The footmen were decked out for the evening in the liveries from ENO's production of *Rozenkavalier*. The organisation of the Rout was presided over by a 'Committee of Honour' of Georgian grandees, like the Earl of March, John Julius Norwich (of course), and the pre-War decorator Jean Monro, but most of the work was done by the young members on the Activities Committee: Charles Hind, Nick John, Henrietta Bredin, James Miller, Sophie Andreae, Alan Powers. The organizing, with its rummaging below stage at ENO, or dealing with the friendly management of the Clermont Club in their William Kent house in Berkeley Square, was nearly as much fun as the Rout itself.

The evening was a riotous success. The guests came to Somerset House after private dinner parties, but were served pudding as we wanted people to arrive by nine pm. Some members gave authentic 'Georgian' dinners, not all of them a success. Glyn managed to lay his guests low with food poisoning by making his 'receipts' too literally Georgian. Sophie Andreae's party came in a horse-drawn carriage which made a terrific *éclat* when it rolled through the arches from the Strand into the courtyard at Somerset House, like The Queen arriving at the Victoria Tower of the Palace of Westminster for the State Opening of Parliament. The clattering hooves and snorting of the horses are a thrillingly authentic Georgian sound. The event was spectacularly gate-crashed by the popular performers, Biddy and Charles, as a Georgian Duchess and her page. Biddy's *tenue* was worthy of Marie Antoinette, especially his towering coiffure.

The whole exercise was to raise money for the Georgian Group's Cleary Fund which makes small grants for restoring eighteenth century buildings and artefacts, such as the Adam shop fronts on Pulteney Bridge in Bath, hatchments in parish churches, or iron railings. Its largest single grant lay in the future when the Cleary Fund paid for the reinstatement of James Wyatt's Carrara marble 'altarpiece' in the Darnley Mausoleum at Cobham in Kent, to ensure that the vandalised interior of that Wyatt masterpiece was fully replicated according to Georgian Group principles and not

19

left as a 'conserve-as-found' gutted shell. I personally gave £3,000 to the Cleary Fund but I do not think any of my colleagues followed suit. (This amount was not as measly thirty-five years ago as it may seem now.)

As part of the 50th anniversary events, Gavin Stamp wrote the history of founding the Group in 1937 by Lord Derwent, Robert Goldring and Robert Byron, author of the *Road to Oxiana* and trenchant critic of philistines. Byron described the Bishop of London, who wanted to demolish some of the Wren churches in the City and sell the sites to Mammon, as 'that mitred serpent'. Byron was killed in the war, but some of the early members were still alive in 1987, including John Summerson at the Soane Museum, the country house architect Claud Phillimore, who had reduced and restored Knowsley and Brocklesby and inherited the Villa Malcontenta from Bertie Landberg in the 1950s. They also included Jim Lees-Milne, a school friend of Robert Byron's and like him, a strong campaigner from the 1930s and '40s and still going strong in the 1980s, publishing his diaries. Gavin and I went to see Jim in Beckford's library in Lansdowne Crescent in Bath where he commuted daily from Badminton to do his writing. He gave us lunch and told us fascinating anecdotes which we included in our history, published by the *Architectural Review*. Gavin photographed me and Jim on the front step of Beckford's house, as past and present Georgian campaigners; and Michael Bloch (Jim's literary executor) used the photo as the frontispiece for one of the volumes of posthumously published diaries. Gavin later enlarged the Group's foundation history and published the more detailed version in the *Georgian Group Journal* in 2012.

When Eleanor Murray retired, having been Secretary of the Georgian Group from the 1950s she was succeeded by Roger White, a trustee who had joined the committee at the same time as Neil Burton in 1981. We were all colleagues at the Historic Buildings Division and

Opposite: Jim Lees-Milne and JMR outside Beckfords front door in Lansdowne Crescent, Bath, in 1987. (Gavin Stamp).

had all three been pupils of Howard Colvin at Oxford. Roger ran the Group while we were based in Spital Square. He was particularly good at organising the outings and activities and upping the Group's scholarly credentials, starting the illustrated *News Letter* for members, and the annual *Georgian Group Journal* in 1992, which publishes serious scholarly articles on Georgian buildings; both the *News Letter* and the *Journal* still flourish and I am still on the Journal's editorial board after twenty-eight years.

The Case Work Committee and case-workers, the Regional Groups, for a time, the Young Georgians, the *Georgian Group Journal*, and the higher calibre activities and educational programme with serious lectures and seminars, were all part of a consistent plan to make the Group more professional and effective, and less of a dilettante, amateur outfit. A good education programme was established for a time, run by a new education officer. When first advertised, Lucy Worsley (later a TV presenter) applied. Having interviewed her, we decided unanimously we could not possibly work with her, it would be like having a permanent Alice in Wonderland in the office! The education revolved round a Georgian dolls house given by a member which was used to teach local children. Steven Parissien became the education officer, and with Neil Burton produced a series of excellent pamphlets on Georgian windows, chimney-pieces etc. to guide people restoring Georgian houses. These are still in print.

When Roger left to write about Georgian garden buildings, which eventually bore fruit in his book on the *Cottage Orné*, he was succeeded by Michael Cudlipp, a scion of the *Daily Mirror* newspaper family. He was 'bonkers'. This became disturbingly apparent by slow degrees. At first it manifested itself in the usual enthusiasm for modernising things, unnecessary updating, and a fetish for bureaucracy, but gradually he became increasingly strange and hectoring. Cudlipp ended up standing at a lectern at the head of the committee table at a meeting of the trustees, while lecturing us on our deficiencies, what he thought we ought to be doing, and the wilder reaches of policy and philosophy. He then had 'a breakdown', and mercifully resigned after a year. We joked that the men in white coats had taken him away. This proved to be truer than we knew. There was a year's gap in his very impressive CV when he came to us.

Gaps in CVs are always worth investigating. In another case I know, not connected with the Georgian Group, it turned out to be the applicant's year in jail. In Cudlipp's case, it turned out to be his year in a mental hospital after he had been sectioned previously. He was succeeded as Secretary by the altogether more sane, competent and effective Neil Burton who was the best Secretary the Georgian Group has had so far. Neil Burton, was another HB colleague and shared my views on strategy: the need for our own headquarters, and a more vigorous campaigning edge to the work as well as a proper educational programme and serious underpinning scholarship. Under Neil, as well as acquiring and developing Fitzroy Square, we instituted more serious conservation focussed weekend events with trips to threatened and damaged Georgian towns like Bristol, Liverpool and Lancaster. The aim was to involve the members more in the charity's preservation work by showing them the problems, and also to support local groups and individuals by flying the flag alongside them. I am not sure if the serious visits of the 1990s were a success with the members who were not used to crunching over broken glass and filthy rubbish in provincial slum streets. They preferred Adam drawing rooms and tea with charming owners. But the joint campaigning did have success for a time, and averted some development horrors, and encouraged the restoration of some buildings which might otherwise have been lost.

The Group from the beginning has always been divided between 'elegant antique dealers' and more down-to-earth campaigning types. This was marked at the foundation, when Peter Derwent, the first chairman, provided glamour and received much of the posthumous credit, while Douglas Goldring's role as the first Secretary, whose hard work really made the Group, has been forgotten; a point Gavin felt about strongly. Bill Harris was succeeded in the 1990s by Jamie Crathorne, one of the Georgian 'antique dealers'. He had worked in a junior capacity at Sotheby's, and later had advised on furnishings for the hotel chain that developed the Royal Crescent Hotel in Bath and Cliveden in Buckinghamshire. He was charming and non-controversial, an English type, good at keeping his head down, and avoiding too much responsibility.

The treasurer during Jamie's time as chairman was a plump South African called Bruce Young. Part of Bruce's supposed expertise and usefulness was his knowledge of computer systems. The early stages of computerisation in English organisations, businesses and the public sector were a nightmare of irrational inefficiency. Computers still are in the official public realm and that of corporate monopolies, though thanks to superior American technology, digitalisation sometimes works and has become useful in the private sector. In the 1990s, small organisations and charities tended to cleave to self-declared 'computer experts' with the naïve faith of African tribes in their witch doctor. Not all computer witch doctors were deserving of the boundless trust they were given as regards the new technology and its budget.

Bruce was not a trustworthy witch doctor; in fact he was criminally dishonest, and took the Georgian Group for a ride. When it became apparent that he was financially 'dodgy' and the computerisation money was going into his own pocket, he was quietly dismissed. He moved on to the Garden History Society, where he did the same thing to them. He then moved on to the Georgian Society of Jamaica and ripped them off. The Jamaican Georgians proved more robust and took him to court. He was convicted of fraud and embezzlement, and died in Wandsworth jail; as far as I know the only Georgian Group Treasurer to do so.

When Jamie Crathorne became Lord Lieutenant of North Yorkshire, he decided that being chairman of the Georgian Group might be too political and he stood down. He nominated Diane Nutting to succeed him. Few members of the committee had ever met her. She was at the time the life tenant of Chicheley Hall, a beautiful early-eighteenth century house near Milton Keynes, designed by Francis Smith of Warwick with panelled rooms, an inlaid oak staircase, and an entrance hall decorated by William Kent.

Diane was devoted to Chicheley, and spent much effort keeping it in repair but sadly could not afford to live there and later surrendered her life-interest to enable it to be sold to the Royal Society which ran it as a conference centre and a three star 'hospitality venue', managed by De Vere Hotels, though they have now put it on the market again. The house lost its magic and she lost her *raison d'être* as its châtelaine. Diane had also served as chairman of the Thames and Chiltern regional committee of the National Trust, and sat on the Royal Fine Art Commission. Chicheley, the National Trust, and Fine Art Commission seemed good qualifications, and she became our chairman with all our support. Our support was not in the end reciprocated. She soon fell out with the Secretary Neil Burton and sacked him. Neil had made little attempt to hide his opinion that he thought her snobbish, ignorant, and rather ridiculous. She in her turn disliked him because on a visit to Chicheley he had put his coffee cup on the carpet beside his chair, as all the tables were too crowded with bibelots and photographs to place anything on them. 'In a house like this,' she exclaimed, unconsciously paraphrasing a favourite operatic line from *Eugene Onegin*.

In Neil's place, she appointed the mysterious Bruno Philip Robert Bargery who did not use his first name but called himself 'Robert'. Bargery had been seconded from the Department of the Environment to be secretary of the Royal Fine Art Commission under Norman St John Stevas, for whom he wrote speeches. Stevas gave him a dazzling reference, and was obviously much infatuated by Bruno's enigmatic smile, deference, and raven black hair (which survived without a hint of grey into his fifties). Stuart Lipton who succeeded Stevas as chairman after the RFAC was reconstituted as CABE (forgive the acronyms), was much more objective and advised us that Bargery would need watching carefully; he 'would not do anything he did not want to do'. Diane, however, shared

Stevas's high opinion and never noticed that Bargery was gradually diversifying the Group from a charity involved in conservation into a vehicle for his own interests, including an estate agency, Georgian Properties, which it was claimed made money for casework, but was outside the Charity Commission's remit. Bruno walked out in a huff a decade or so later, when the trustees refused his request to invest in the Georgian estate agency as it was not a permitted use of charitable funds

Diane herself had resigned a year earlier and stormed out as chairman, melodramatically shaking her fist and shouting 'You *shut* up!' and 'I will get *you*!' at trustees, before slamming the Georgian panelled doors behind her in a diminuendo of crashes as she rushed from the building to her third-hand Bentley in the square outside. She was replaced, after an ineffective interim, by two good chairmen in succession, an excellent treasurer, new trustees and a competent secretary. All is well once more with the Georgian Group.

The Georgian Group in the 1980s and 1990s was only one prong of my continued campaigning to preserve the historic buildings, places and landscapes. After the GLC and, with it, the Historic Buildings Committee, was abolished in 1986, the staff were given the option of transferring to a new London department of English Heritage or taking their leave. Several colleagues left and established their own businesses. Thus Bob Weston set up his own firm Hamilton Weston, reproducing historic wallpapers. John Sambrook became the leading manufacturer of Georgian fan lights using wrought iron frames and cast lead ornament, a technique he taught himself. The firm still flourishes, though John died a decade or so ago. Thus, specialist expertise which had been a service of public benefit, was commercialised. I toyed with a similar thought of privatising myself. Lancastrian business genes have always given me a sense of admiration for entrepreneurial activity, but I postponed the plunge for two years.

Some of Bob Weston's wallpapers were used for the bedrooms in my house at Barbon, and I installed one of John Sambrook's elegant fanlights in the pair of 1820s Georgian houses which I restored—reinstating glazing bars and iron railings—as offices in the Fishergate Hill conservation area of Preston. (This was part of the property that has come down to me from my great-grandfather like the terrible shops and flats in Central Drive, Blackpool, the remnant of the Bloomfield estate, which my family laid out and developed in 1895, and Hill Top Farm at Whittle which had been retained when the quarry there was sold in 1930.) John delivered the fanlight to Doughty Mews in London. I took it north on the train from Euston, despite its weight, and arranged for my Lancashire builder to collect it on the platform at Preston station, before continuing the journey to Lancaster and Barbon. I was the only person on the West Coast train that day travelling with a fanlight. I thought, what limited lives other people must have. They don't even bring fanlights with them on the train.

I mistakenly decided to transfer to English Heritage in 1986 for the short-term, as there were a number of interesting schemes in Westminster, especially Jacob Rothschild's restoration of Spencer House, which I wanted to see through to the finish, and wrote the guide book when it opened. Already, however, we could see the way things were going. Management consultants were causing havoc throughout the Civil Service and quangocracy in the late-1980s, aligning them with failed 1960s 'management', structures and functions, with emphasis on gender-neutral box ticking diversity, 'equal opportunities', the promotion of red tape, clumsy computerisation, and all the rest of it (competence was not a criterion). Thus was created the magnificent Rolls Royce machine, staffed with efficient, highly educated people, which was to handle in the years to come the Foot and Mouth epidemic in 2001, the 2008 banking crisis, Brexit, 2016-2020, and the Covid health scare 2020, with such strategic brilliance, informed understanding, and intelligent grasp of detail.

After two years, it was time to jump ship. Joseph Friedman (one of the many clever pupils of David Watkin at Cambridge) suggested setting up a historic buildings consultancy. Joe was busy

David Watkin, Professor of Architectural History at Cambridge. For many years JMRs co-vice-chairman of the Georgian Group and joint trustee of 6 Fitzroy Square, the Group's Headquarters.

cataloguing the contents of the Duchess of Windsor's house in the Bois de Boulogne in Paris for Mr Fayed of Harrods notoriety. Joe was a contemporary of Tom Helme, who had become interiors advisor to the National Trust and they had worked together researching the historic decoration at James Wyatt's Castle Coole in Northern Ireland, which attracted some publicity with its discovery of 'Germolene pink'. The idea was that we should all three go into business together as a consultancy, combining our shared expertise, Tom in interior decoration, Joe on contents, furniture and art, and me on historic architecture and planning. We did one job together, the restoration of the Siena marbled Nash decorative scheme in the central hall of the former United Services Club in

Waterloo Place, which had become the headquarters of the Institute of Directors. Tom, however, became involved in a paint company purveying authentic historic colours, Farrow and Ball. He hit the jackpot and created a national brand which earned him millions when it was sold. Joe and I formed a business partnership, Historic Buildings Consultants, on our own in 1988 and worked together for a decade on many fascinating jobs, including the locations for Merchant Ivory films. Eventually Joe decided to concentrate entirely on his interests in the art market and associated consultancy, and set up his own company, Joseph Friedman Ltd., specialising in that aspect. I continued to work as a consultant on historic building and restoration, from a little office at Doughty Mews, but co-operating with private owners and a range of architects and designers in a flexible freelance way. Such a way of working fitted well with all my other interests and occupations, and continued through the 1990s and into the twenty-first century; working with Civic Design Partnership on award-winning conservation plans for Seven Dials and Covent Garden, with Craig Hamilton on several of his new classical houses and chapels, John Simpson with his buildings for educational clients, William Bertram of Bath on a range of country houses, Charles Blackett Ord on the initial project to save the shell of Lowther Castle in Westmorland, and many similar schemes. Such projects have been extraordinarily interesting and enabled me to earn a civilised living while giving scope for my own special interests and limited abilities. I often think, thank god, I did not become a chartered accountant, as advised to do by all the careers specialists. I was saved from that by not being able to count above ten, and taking three goes to pass Maths 'O' level back in 1964. Failure is often the gate to human contentment.